Gilbert Cesbron

Chiens perdus sans collier

Marie Cardinal

La Clé sur la porte

Colin Roberts

Senior Lecturer in French,
Coventry Polytechnic

University of Glasgow French and German Publications

1988

University of Glasgow French and German Publications

Series Editors: Mark G. Ward (German)
                  Geoff Woollen (French)

Consultant Editors : Colin Smethurst
                     Kenneth Varty

Modern Languages Building, University of Glasgow,
Glasgow G12 8QL, Scotland.

First published 1988

Printed by Glasgow University Printing Department.

ISBN   0 85261 249 4

CONTENTS

This book is dedicated to my mother

ACKNOWLEDGMENTS

I would like to thank Dr. Anne Baroian, of the National University of Iran, for helping me obtain biographical information on both authors and for a number of helpful suggestions. My thanks also go to my colleague John Wright, of the Department of Language Studies at Coventry Polytechnic, for his careful reading of this study at manuscript stage and for his constructive comments. I would also like to record my gratitude to Geoff Woollen, the series editor. Page references to *Chiens perdus sans collier* and to *La Clé sur la porte* are taken from the "J'ai lu" and Livre de Poche editions respectively.

Coventry, August 1988   Colin J. Roberts

ACKNOWLEDGEMENTS

I would like to thank the manufacturers of the various PLCs for supplying information about the material covered in the book...

Coventry, August 1988

Chiens Perdus sans collier

Gilbert Cesbron: life and work

Gilbert Cesbron (the pseudonym of Jean Guyon) was born in Paris in 1913. After studying at the Lycée Condorcet he went on to the Ecole des sciences politiques. He worked in radio while at the same time pursuing his career as a writer and, from 1972, devoted himself to charity work. He published more than fifty works, which were well received by the public, as well as hundreds of articles on contemporary problems. One of his first, *Les Innocents de Paris* (1944) was much admired by the writer Colette and was awarded the Prix de la Guilde du livre. Ten other novels were awarded prizes, of which the most notable was the Prix Sainte-Beuve for *Notre prison est un royaume* (1948). His most famous play, *Il est minuit , docteur Schweitzer* (1952), was adapted for radio and made into a film starring Jeanne Moreau in the role of Mlle. Marie.

Cesbron's works tackle moral issues: for example, euthanasia in *Il est plus tard que tu ne penses* (1958) and violence in *Entre chiens et loups* (1962). He adopts a resolutely Christian perspective on society's problems and in *Libérez Barabbas* (1957) he poses one of the fundamental questions facing the European conscience: is it possible for a bourgeois to be a Christian ? Cesbron presents in his novels a compassionate portrayal of the human misery, suffering and humiliation of the underprivileged. His populist approach to problems is combined with a very literary style, and his choice of subjects has appealed to readers. However, his work has not always been well received by the critics, who have accused him of being melodramatic and mawkish in his treatment of characters and situations. When he stood for the Académie Française in 1963 he was not elected.

Cesbron belongs to a tradition of Catholic writers who fuse their Christian faith with their writing: Julien Green, Charles Péguy, Georges Bernanos and François Mauriac. Each of his novels tends to illustrate a contemporary problem. Cesbron always rejected the label "Catholic writer" because he was wary of proselytism. His obituary in *Le Monde* of 14

3

August 1979 quotes him as saying that he preferred to consider himself as 'un chrétien qui écrit des livres pour aider les autres à vivre.' It also records that he was a generous man who gave away part of his book royalties to charity. He was a regular visitor at the hospital of La Salpêtrière in Paris, where he comforted the incurably sick, and was also a regular prison visitor. In 1972 he became Secretary General of the Catholic charity, Secours Catholique. He had to leave after a year because of ill health.

Chiens perdus sans collier was published in 1954. The film of the book starred Jean Gabin in the role of Lamy, the Juge des Enfants. Directed by Jean Delannoy, it was shown at the Venice film festival of 1955. The challenges and risks of childhood, which is the subject of the novel, are a recurring theme in Cesbron's work. Monique Detry, in her study of Cesbron, quotes him as saying: 'Enfant, guide d'enfants, c'est moi.' [1] He is deeply concerned about the present-day treatment of children, and blames the modern media, in particular, for doing them great harm by undermining traditional values. Cesbron is convinced that there exists a wall between children and adults. It is the division that exists between the spirit of curiosity and adventure on the one hand, and self-satisfaction and fear of change on the other. The spirit of childhood, which combines loyalty with wholehearted commitment, confidence and hope, is a necessary antidote to the widespread cynicism of society.

The two young heroes of *Chiens perdus sans collier* are called Alain and Marc. The significance of the novel's title is conveyed by the opening pages, when Alain sees a stray dog without a collar weaving its way through traffic in the centre of Paris. Tired and confused, the wretched animal is ready to let itself be captured and taken by policemen to the pound where, unless it is claimed, it will be put down. To save the dog Alain pretends to be its owner. He produces a piece of string which he hopes will pass for a dog lead, but the policemen see through his pathetic gesture of help. The situation is saved, however, by an Alsatian which suddenly comes to the rescue. The crucial point of the scene is that Alain instinctively identifies with the 'chien perdu' because he too feels alone and vulnerable. An implicit comparison is drawn between stray dogs and orphans. Indeed, the recurring image of the stray dog is used by the author as a <u>symbol</u> of the deprived child. Just as a dog needs a good master, so a child needs the protection, guidance and above all love of its parents. When a child is without parents or is abused by them, society has to intervene in the form of doctors, magistrates, social workers and others. The novel depicts in a favourable light the dedicated and effective work of such professionals in child welfare, but it paints a less sanguine picture of how children in care are regarded by members of the general public. The auxiliary accompanying Alain says that stray dogs have to be impounded because 'des chiens perdus, c'est dangereux pour l'ordre'(p. 9). In the face of a hostile world one dog helps another. Likewise Alain and Marc find in each other's company mutual support and friendship when their lives are drawn together in the children's home. Cesbron writes:

> Sauvés parce qu'ils sont deux... Mais le secret des chiens perdus sans collier n'est-il pas aussi celui des enfants abandonnés? Alain Robert ne sait pas qu'en ce moment même, de l'autre côté de cette ville inconnue, Marc s'apprête à le rejoindre. Marc... —mais patience! Le Destin qui conduit l'un vers l'autre les enfants perdus, le Destin souriant a deux mains: sa droite, la plus habile, s'appelle le Médecin; sa gauche, celle du cœur, le Juge des enfants.'Sauvés parce qu'ils sont deux...'(p. 10)

Alain sees the stray dog while he is being taken to the children's hospital at Denfert-Rochereau. On arrival he is submitted to a medical examination. A letter to the hospital director describes his wayward behaviour. There are a number of scene changes: we eavesdrop on a meeting of the National Commission for Child Welfare and on an interview in the hospital between Alain and Dr. Clérant, the child psychologist. There follows a case conference involving social workers chaired by Dr. Clérant.

In Chapter II, Lamy meets Darrier, a young lawyer who visits the homes of delinquent and deprived children on a voluntary basis. Darrier understands the importance of the local gang as a focus of loyalty as well as the difficulties facing children in rough neighbourhoods like Les Carrières. He keeps a rendezvous with young volunteer helpers who work under his direction and confronts the gang leader, Pierre Merlerin, nicknamed 'le Caïd'. Darrier has been helping members of the gang find premises for a clubhouse and, despite opposition from local people, including a church group, their efforts are eventually rewarded. A house-warming party is

5

organised, and in order to provide his share of the food, Marc is forced to steal some apples. He is taken away by the police and despatched to the children's home at Terneray; this has the effect of removing him from Merlerin's bad influence, which Lamy had forbidden Darrier to do without due cause. Ironically, the latter too will soon end up at Terneray.

Chapters III to VI describe life at Terneray. The reader is introduced to the staff, who discuss their work and criticise the goverment's child welfare programme. Sunday is the day when parents visit their children, and on one such occasion Lamy and Doublet, the deputy magistrate, appear. Sundays are distressing for the orphans because they are reminded that they have no parents. A fight breaks out between them and the other boys. It is stopped by one of the staff, called Tomawak, who berates the youngsters for their stupidity and underlines their need to stick together to overcome the social disabilities they will have to face in life. One of the orphans, Olaf, runs away on a cold winter's night because he wants to imitate his hero, Tarzan. He eventually dies in hospital from the effects of exposure to the cold.

Chapters VII to X cover the separate escapes from Terneray of Alain, Marc and then Alain for the second time. The idea of running away first comes to Alain while visiting Olaf in hospital. His plan succeeds, and at the same time he frees a dog called Caddy who is being kept as a medical guinea-pig. Once again, as in the opening scene, Alain comes to the defence of a weak and vulnerable creature. He is eventually found sleeping rough in Paris. The police suspect him of complicity in a bank robbery and he is detained in a hospice for the old, infirm and incurable. After the police are satisfied that he is innocent, he is briefly returned to the hospital at Denfert-Rochereau. However, by running away he has committed a juvenile offence and has to appear in court before Lamy and Doublet. Back at Terneray other boys, including Marc, also decide to run away. They steal a car belonging to one of the staff and in the course of their escape the ringleader, Paulo, knocks out another. After a day in Paris visiting his family and friends, Marc goes to Lamy's home. Lamy is out but Marc is welcomed in by his son. When Lamy returns he listens sympathetically to what Marc has to say and goes to Terneray to explain what had happened. On the way he comes across Alain, who has run away yet again in order to find Marc.

In the final chapter the instigators are punished. Merlerin is sent to a youth rehabilitation scheme and Paulo is sent to borstal. The story reaches an emotional climax, with Darrier pleading in court before Lamy and Doublet for Marc to be returned to his parents. The novel ends with Lamy clearing his desk. He is leaving the Juvenile Magistrate's Bench for a new job in the Appeal Court. He is aware that there is little more he can do for children in care, but 'il n'en éprouvait aucune satisfaction. Il le ressentait plutôt comme un aveu d'impuissance que comme la certitude du devoir accompli'(p. 312).

Child deprivation and delinquency in France

Chiens perdus sans collier contains information on the postwar numbers of children in need. During the meeting of the Commission to decide on the budget to be allotted to child welfare, Dr. Clérant says that the war has left 28,000 children in care in France, many in a deplorable physical condition. Lamy informs the meeting that there are 230 million undernourished children in the world, 13 million abandoned throughout Europe and, in France alone, two million are suffering from the effects of the war (pp. 27 and 29). He notes that, in Paris, there are 30,000 latchkey children and bewails the fact that it has taken years to obtain from the French bureaucracy 'que les gosses ne nous soient plus amenés menottes aux mains'(p. 30). Cesbron describes the woeful inability of the French bureaucracy in the postwar period to get to grips with the urgent problem of child welfare. Delinquents as well as backward and sick children are all lumped together. The Ministries of Justice, Health and Education are ready, in principle, to assume responsibility for children, but lack resources.

In the nineteenth century, juvenile crime was a major social problem. Of those who appeared before the courts, between 15% and 18% were minors.[2] The tendency of some young people to drift into crime at an early age was first underlined in a report of 1831. Minors were not considered responsible in law for their actions unless it could be proved that they were fully aware of the consequences of their misdeeds. The courts attempted to distinguish between children who were malicious and those who were victims of circumstance. The intention of the law was to treat delinquents with severity while at the same time trying to rehabilitate them through education. In practice, the penal system stressed severity and only lip service was paid to the benefits of re-education. The age of minority was raised from sixteen to eighteen in 1906; those under the age of thirteen were declared irresponsible in law in 1912; and in 1945 the age for this was raised to eighteen.

In the 1960s it was established that orphans constituted one third of juvenile recidivists. The number may well have been higher in the nineteenth century. The separate detention of children and adults was stipulated in the law of 1850. Emphasis was placed on children's "moral, religious and professional education". Children were sent to penitentiary colonies in the countryside, an example of which can be found in Alphonse Daudet's novel *Jack* (1876).[3] It was hoped that the moral character of young delinquents from the slums would be improved by immersing them in pastoral surroundings, but many resented compulsory agricultural labour and grew actively to dislike the countryside. An increasingly military discipline was introduced into the colonies, which simply served to isolate young offenders from the rest of society.

Violence has increased considerably since the early 1970s. Whereas mainly seventeen- to eighteen-year-olds were involved in burglaries twenty-five years ago, now there are growing numbers of younger children. Violence is still mainly confined to young males. A 1977 report, chaired by Alain Peyrefitte, the Minister of Justice, found that of those involved in violence, 94.9% were boys and only 5.1% were girls. [4] It is also a group phenomenon. The same report found that 73% of offences were committed by gangs of youths as opposed to youths acting individually. The younger the age group, the more powerful the group psychosis, with 85 to 95% of those between nine and twelve convicted of violent offences acting in a group. The Peyrefitte report found that 24% of those involved in hold-ups were under twenty. Many elderly French people are afraid of the young. Three out of four think that young people are more likely than adults to use violence. Fear of juvenile delinquents increases with age, and there is every reason to believe that the hostility of Doublet, the Deputy Magistrate, towards young offenders is still representative of large sections of public

8

opinion in France today.

The breakdown of the family unit and lack of communication between parents and children are, of course, major contributory factors in delinquency. New developments, run-down council estates and high-rise flats, often built on the outskirts of cities and with poor amenities, are all conducive to the growth of delinquency. The influence of cinema and especially television has also been blamed. In the early 1950s, when the action takes place, television sets were quite rare. This is not the case today and the Peyrefitte report records that 20% of television programmes are devoted to violence and that the same percentage of characters in films shown on French television are criminals. The boys in the novel are influenced by cinema stereotypes. For example, when the police come for Marc at the youth club, he imagines he is a film gangster being led away by the "cops".

Juvenile gangs

Children from slum areas who are forced on to the streets because of problems in the home are likely to meet with rejection from the community at large and be subject to increased police surveillance. This is likely only to fuel their sense of frustration and resentment. They tend to congregate in gangs and express their alienation from society by surrounding their activities with an air of conspiracy. Each gang has its own lair, where members gather away from the prying eyes of adults. Marc's meets in a factory basement. The group regulates the behaviour of its members through the imposition of its own code of honour which sets it apart from the rest of society. Thus Marc is made to swear an oath of loyalty to the gang leader, Pierre Merlerin.

In 1960, a study was made by a team of American and French sociologists of Parisian juvenile gangs. [5] It is close enough in time to the period when the novel is set to be of particular help in understanding the milieu of Marc and the other boys. It is not surprising that Cesbron focusses on boys, because most delinquents are male. The study found that delinquents are often either orphans or come from broken and unhappy homes. A number of factors determine patterns of violence and antisocial behaviour in a big city like Paris. There is, first of all, the existence of slum areas on the outskirts of the city. Marc comes from such an area. Schooling is a low priority for slum boys and their families. Most leave school early. When the novel was written, the minimum school leaving age in France was fourteen; now it is sixteen. Those who show academic ability are discouraged by their families from pursuing their studies, and truancy is condoned or ignored. In contrast to this, children of middle-class parents are encouraged to value education and to defer gratification rather than start work early and earn money. When the 1960 field study was conducted, unemployment was a serious problem among delinquents who had left school early. It is, if anything, an even greater problem in the 1980s, since the recession has led to record levels of unemployment which have hit the youngest and least skilled the hardest. The low level of education of slum children does not equip them adequately for work, and they are only able to obtain low-skilled jobs, which are poorly paid and monotonous. They do not look to the future and have no long-term goals. Their idea of success is limited to objectives that are immediate, tangible and occasionally risky.

The study found that the size, age and organisation of juvenile gangs in Paris vary. Numbers range from five to twenty. There are a dozen in Marc's gang. Each one has its own territory, but in areas where Parisian gangs operate they are not normally linked to organised crime. They also tend to be smaller and more loosely structured than their American counterparts, and the struggle for status is less keenly felt. Among working-class French adolescents it was found that, unlike among their American opposite numbers, there were relatively few cases of drug addiction in 1960. At that time drug taking was confined to a small number of middle-class youths. It is significant that there is no mention of drugs in the novel. Today, however, the drug habit has spread to every layer of French society. The rise in the number of youths convicted of burglary and other offences in recent years is partly due to the growth of drug addiction which forces addicts to turn to crime to pay for their habit.

Quite predictably, the study established that younger boys learn from older ones and that this helps to integrate different juvenile age groups. As a result, gangs gain in stability and coherence. In the absence of a stable

10

home and of parental authority, gang members emulate the values and conduct of their peer group. The gang acts as a surrogate family. Paulo and Merlerin want to escape from Terneray to be with their friends rather than with their families. Because professional criminals keep delinquent gangs at arm's length, juvenile delinquents do not automatically aspire to or envisage a criminal career for themselves. However, the slum districts they tend to come from have high numbers of petty criminals and this offers youngsters the contacts, knowledge and opportunity to take part in minor illegal activities. The study found that the sort of offences for which Parisian delinquents are convicted are sex offences, assaulting adults, armed hold-ups, and even bank robbery. Obviously Cesbron does not consider that he is stretching the reader's credibility when he has Alain detained by the police on suspicion of complicity in the latter. However, most convictions are for offences against property. During the war years and in the immediate postwar period of rationing and shortages, offences against property were rife, with stolen objects finding their way on to the black market. The study concluded that a crucial factor in steering gang boys in France away from delinquency is military service, which occurs at just the age when the delinquent is on the threshold of manhood. Two years' military service, often spent abroad, removes the young person from his delinquent environment. On his return to civilian life, the prospect of work, marriage and new family commitments changes his outlook.

The Child Welfare Services

Minors convicted of serious offences, like Paulo, are sent to borstals or *internats pénitentiaires* . Minors taken into care are sent to homes which are run either by the State or by private charities. Girls who are pregnant are sent to maternity homes. The staff in children's homes fall into three groups. Firstly, there are those who are administrators; secondly, there are trained teachers who are able to teach basic subjects and equip youngsters for a trade; finally there are those, known as *éducateurs* , who look after and supervise the children on a daily basis. The *baccalauréat* plus a teaching certificate or a university degree is required of the first group. Those in the second group have to be qualified teachers and to have the necessary qualifications in the technical subject they teach. A *baccalauréat* and a vocation for working with problem children qualify the third category.

The novel highlights two major problems confronting the Child Welfare Services. Firstly, there is the danger of making the job of *éducateur* too career-oriented. Provins, the Regional Director of Child Welfare, concedes that those who work with children need job security and a proper career structure. But this can lead to the danger of men and women being attracted to the job for the wrong reasons: because it offers security rather than a way of following a vocation.'L'âge héroïque est fini! Des pionniers qui vieillissent, c'est lamentable...', exclaims Provins (p. 78). He opines that as soon as the authorities issue a new education decree governing the terms and conditions of service of *éducateurs* , there will be a flood of applicants. An influx of careerists means that the children's homes will risk losing the dedicated service of those who have a genuine vocation. The *éducateurs* who have been some time at Terneray disapprove of their new colleague, Robert, because he holds the *baccalauréat* and has no real empathy for children. It is almost as if, in their eyes, his academic qualifications set up a barrier between him and the children in his care.

The second danger confronting those involved in child care arises from the burgeoning bureaucracy of the Social Services, which creates a widening gap between those who make decisions at the top and those who work with children on the ground. This is graphically illustrated in the course of the meeting of the Commission on Child Welfare, bringing together representatives from different government departments and from the medical and legal professions. The meeting is conducted like a game of bridge, with committee members scoring points off each other. Discussion revolves around financial resources, and the realities of child deprivation, which are meant to be the object of their deliberations, seem forgotten. Ministries issue circulars and recommendations, but these have to be interpreted on the spot by those directly concerned. Provins recalls that he was given money to build a workshop tower. He used the money instead to build a children's home because, in his judgement, it was more important to save twenty children than to train, a year ahead of time, a team of milling-machine turners. Provins is worried about the growing involvement of the State in welfare work. He is concerned that, after creating a new *statut d'éducateur* , it will attempt to exclude voluntary agencies from child welfare. The State is spreading its tentacles, according to Provins, not out of greed or ambition but because it is driven to do so by the very momentum its own power of patronage generates: 'l'Etat reste tout bête, avec les légions d'honneur dans une main, ses sinécures dans l'autre, personne n'en veut! Alors, il s'affole: vite, un statut! des contrôleurs! des papiers, des papiers, vite!'(p. 81) The growth of the Welfare State—a comprehensive social security system was introduced in 1945—was seen as a threat to the continued involvement of private, often Catholic charities in the field of child welfare. Because of his Catholicism, some of these fears inform Cesbron's attitude to State monopoly of welfare.

In France, the need for specialised child welfare workers to help integrate delinquent children into society has been recognised. A decree issued in 1972 gave official sanction to *clubs et équipes de prévention* . These were born out of an experiment that dates back to the immediate postwar years. At the time the novel was written, the Social Services were far less developed than they are today. There were fewer social workers and these only became involved once an offence had been committed. What was required was a strategy of prevention. At the time, the courts had to rely on charities or individuals acting in a voluntary capacity, like the lawyer Darrier. Darrier takes on an impossible task. He is treated with suspicion by the working-class slum boys he befriends because they see him as a middle-class, professional "do-gooder". Moreover, it is not simply the boys themselves, whether individually or as a group, who need to be made to feel part of society, but their families, communities and localities too. This is a massive task, calling for a sustained effort by government to tackle the social, educational and infrastructural problems of slum areas. The concept of *club et équipe de prévention* , though not a complete answer in itself, does go some way towards plugging the holes. In some respects, Darrier and the group of volunteer helpers he gathers around him constitute a pioneer model of what an *équipe de prévention* should be. Together they encourage local boys from Marc's district of Les Carrières to find premises for a clubhouse. Darrier does not provide money but he helps them cut through red tape.The object of the exercise is to get youngsters who might otherwise have turned to petty crime to undertake work that suits their needs and, by so doing, to enhance the quality of life of their communities. Ideally those involved in the scheme should live and work in the area, although the strain of living in a slum district with a high level of violence might prove too great over a long period.

The Peyrefitte report found that *éducateurs de prévention* need to be given prospects of career advancement and development through in-service training. Some *éducateurs* have been brought up in slum areas themselves and, by dint of personal example, are able to dissuade the youths in their care from a life of delinquency. Darrier's helpers are examples of voluntary *éducateurs* . They share the background of the boys they befriend; they know their lives and difficulties more intimately than Darrier ever can because they live in the area and are not identified as middle-class. It must not be forgotten that class consciousness is particularly strong in a socially conservative country like France, where there is less opportunity for upward social mobility than in the United States, for example. If this is true today, it was far more so in the early 1950s when the novel was written. The working-class boys Cesbron portrays are suspicious of the bourgeoisie and immured in a ghetto mentality. In fact Vémard, the communist director of a rehabilitation scheme for delinquents, sees this as a source of strength and tries to reinforce the class identity of those boys who are referred to him.

The *Juge des Enfants*

France was one of the first countries to recognise that young offenders had to be treated differently from adults. The penal code of 1810 established a rule, limited to sixteen-year-olds, allowing the courts discretion to deal leniently with minors. They could either discharge the child, on the grounds that he did not realise the seriousness of the offence, or they could take into account all the extenuating circumstances. In practice, though, severity was the order of the day. Nowadays, cases are dealt with either by an Examining Magistrate (Juge d'Instruction) or by a Juvenile Magistrate (Juge des Enfants). The category of Juvenile Magistrate, modelled on the Belgian

14

system, was created in 1945. Unlike the Examining Magistrate, the Juvenile Magistrate specialises in cases involving children. The law of 1 October 1945 allowed for the setting up of special courts to deal with minors. It also emphasised rehabilitation rather than punishment. The intention was that all cases should be investigated by a Juvenile Magistrate. He (or she) is also responsible for monitoring the rehabilitation of the young offender and for dealing with his family. In addition, where social conditions in a particular district have deteriorated, making rehabilitation almost impossible, he is responsible for informing the authorities so that appropriate measures can be taken. He is also in constant touch with the Child Welfare Services. Lamy's ideal is that all cases involving delinquents should be handed over to the Juvenile Magistrate. In recent years, however, more and more cases involving delinquents have been dealt with by ordinary courts sitting in special juvenile sessions, with Examining Magistrates presiding. Since the latter are not involved on a day to day basis with child welfare, the interests of the child are not always well served. From 1959 to 1975, for example, the number of sentences handed down, in proportion to the number of delinquent minors who appeared before the courts, increased from 15% to 32%. The inference of the Peyrefitte report is that Examining Magistrates prefer punishment to re-education, and it recommends that all minors should be dealt with by Juvenile Magistrates instead.

The authority of the Juvenile Magistrate has suffered in recent years from the growth of the Social Services and their increasing organisation and rationalisation. The responsibility for removing the child from its parents is shared by a number of agencies, and this can work against the interests of parents and child since it is difficult to know against whom to lodge an appeal. Of course parents too may ask for their children to be taken into care. Sometimes they do so simply in order to off-load on to the State the cost of the child's upbringing, as Lamy points out (p. 224). In the early 1950s, when the novel was written, the Juvenile Magistrate enjoyed more independence, and hence more authority, precisely because the organisation of the Social Services was more rudimentary than it is today. The police have eroded his position in recent years by visiting offenders at home and becoming more involved in rehabilitation. This is not strictly their function, and can lead to delinquents and their families confusing the roles of the police and the Social Services. The Peyrefitte report calls for both an increase in the number of Juvenile Magistrates and for them to be transferred less frequently. Only by remaining in their job sufficiently long can they ensure coherence and continuity of action and become fully acquainted with the Child Welfare Services in their area. Significantly, when Lamy is transferred to the Appeal Court, the reader is left with the clear impression that this is detrimental to the Juvenile Bench. Provins reacts by calling it 'la journée des mauvaises nouvelles '(p. 257).

The Juvenile Magistrate is not simply concerned with ascertaining the facts of the case. He must also take into account the accused's background and moral character. Social workers draw up a report on the child, which includes all information relevant to an understanding of his environment, the relevant facts of his life, his parent's occupations and habits, the way he has been brought up and looked after, and the opinions of neighbours, friends and teachers. No doubt Cesbron does not include school teachers among his adult characters because school is not an important focus of social life for the boys he depicts. The investigation also pays particular attention to any history of family illness, whether physical or mental, and a doctor and a psychiatrist must examine the accused. Prior to the trial, minors may be kept in protective custody, but the law of 5 August 1850 stipulates that they must not be detained with adults. Alain's detention in a hospice for the old and incurably sick is hardly an improvement, one might think, on an adult prison! The public are excluded from juvenile courts: only witnesses, near relatives of the accused, guardians, barristers, social workers and, with the court's permission, representatives of charities and other organisations involved in child welfare may attend. Members of the press may be present in certain circumstances.

In cases of vagrancy, incitement to immorality, lack of care and neglect of education and material well-being, the court can withdraw parental rights. Thus Lamy has Marc sent to a home, although he does so with the parents' agreement. However, the threat of custody is often enough to bring about an improvement, and social workers help by visiting and advising parents. By supporting families in difficulties, the Juvenile Magistrate, in tandem with the Social Services, can prevent children being taken into custody. In the immediate postwar period, in the Paris area alone, more than 10,000

16

children were examined regularly by psychiatrists and doctors.[6]

The French system of dealing with delinquents has been accused of being too judicial. This is one of the main criticisms of Lamy, who feels that the closed bourgeois mentality of the Bench militates against the interests of the child. He calls for a permanent staff of Juvenile Magistrates who are thoroughly experienced in dealing with delinquents, and for the setting up of a special Juvenile Magistrate's court which would be concerned with the rehabilitation of the offender. Doublet, who has a narrow view of the Juvenile Magistrate's role, puts the emphasis on punishment. By bringing all cases involving minors before special children's courts, presided over by a Juvenile Magistrate, Lamy hopes that there will be a better liaison between the court, social workers, children's homes and borstals. In addition, it would allow more time and expertise to be given to the choice of the best institution to which to send the young person. For Lamy, the treatment of delinquency has to be removed as far as possible from the legal sphere and placed in a broader social context.

A Portrait of child deprivation

It has been said of deprived children that 'their deprivation seems to express itself in a well-marked indifference to everybody but themselves.'[7] The first impression we are given of Alain is of a boy who is sullen and hostile to adults. His hostility is born of fear and distrust. He accompanies impassively the auxiliary who takes him to the children's hospital at Denfert-Rochereau. He never blinks, his hands are plunged in his pockets, he remains silent, appears uninterested in the world around him and makes the social worker uneasy. There is a psychological barrier between Alain and his minder which seems insurmountable. For Alain, grown-ups belong to an alien world and his adult companion is barely human in his eyes, 'un monument parmi les autres '(p. 6). The coldness and hostility of the adult world is reinforced by the atmosphere at the hospital at Denfert-Rochereau. Alain is suspicious of the reception he receives from the doctors and nurses. Their warm welcome is simply 'le piège préféré des grandes personnes'(p. 13). Alain's file describes him as secretive, rarely smiling, never opening

17

up. It records that he stopped speaking to his foster parents, played truant, was listless at school, looked for fights and was indifferent to punishment; he adopted a "couldn't-care-less" attitude at home, lost all notion of time and became a compulsive liar; he deliberately scratched the bodywork of a car belonging to his foster parents and destroyed family souvenirs; his cantankerous behaviour continued with other couples who fostered him; he let animals loose on the farm of one set of foster parents, disappeared for three days while staying with another, went on hunger strike while staying with yet another; indeed, the report concludes, he had acquired a 'réputation détestable'(p. 22). His unfriendly and even hostile behaviour continues when he is visited at Terneray by the Deroux couple, who want to adopt him. He tells them that he detests them and runs away. Alain presents all the signs of emotional deprivation: listlessness, secretiveness, a distressing inability to communicate, truancy, aggression, lying, hostility and wilful destructiveness.

The outward indifference of the deprived child conceals vulnerability in the face of a hostile world. Alain's own vulnerability is brought home to him at the hospital at Denfert-Rochereau. He is made to feel like an entry in a file, an item to be processed, a case number and not a person in his own right. His sense of helplessness is underlined by the sarcastic repetition of the language of bureaucracy. To the hospital administration, Alain's life is contained in his dossier which becomes 'un compagnon inséparable'(p. 14). It is even more indispensable than Alain himself. Children awaiting their turn to be medically examined have 'des yeux tristes et résignés, comme les bêtes d'une étable'(p. 15).

The deprived child finds it difficult to give and receive love, thereby sparking off a vicious cycle of loneliness and emotional frustration. When Alain arrives at Terneray, he is cold-shouldered by the other boys and thinks to himself: 'Je m'en fous, puisque je les emmerde'(p. 15). He throws up a wall around himself as a form of protection and appears as 'dur, froid, aveugle et sourd comme une pierre'(p. 16). Alain cannot show affection because he has not learned to trust other people, not even foster parents. He feels resentment that the Deroux couple only see him as a poor substitute for their own son. They do not love him for himself and he experiences self-loathing and insecurity.

Emotionally deprived children thirst for love, but the affection they get from adults carries its own risks. Françoise, for example, one of the *éducatrices* at Terneray, inadvertently hurts Alain, who has grown to love her. Cesbron returns again and again to the theme of wounded love. All those closely involved with deprived children—psychiatrists, nurses, social workers, magistrates and voluntary helpers—are aware of the danger and they respond to it in different ways. Clérant counsels caution and distance. When Lamy asks him why he adopts a cool manner with children, he replies that he is not being cold, but objective. He argues that adults must avoid being over-friendly and refrain from showing pity, because deprived children have to adapt to life without close and warm family ties. The psychiatrist acts as a mirror enabling children to see themselves face to face. On another occasion, Clérant picks up Alain when he faints after running away from the Deroux couple who came to visit him at Terneray. He takes the opportunity to warn Françoise not to get too close to Alain. Clérant tells her: 'Pour Alain Robert, il ne s'agit pas de remplacer sa mère, *mais de le former à l'idée de vivre sans mère* '(p. 139). The novel charts the emotionally fraught relationship between Françoise and Alain. When Alain asks to stay with her instead of going to see a Tarzan film with the other boys, she heeds Clérant's warning and tells Alain to go and see the film. He leaves before the end in order to be with her, but he senses her unease at his return and says '*chaque fois que j'ai aimé quelqu'un il m' a abandonné* '(p. 166). Significantly, they read together in Saint-Exupéry's *Le Petit Prince* the tale of the fox tamed by the Prince, who eventually has to abandon it. The pain and fear of rejection are reflected in the boy's prematurely aged face and the author comments that Françoise 'fut presque effrayée par sa dureté, par ses rides d'homme'(p. 166). Lamy's problem is different to Françoise's. He is conscious that his dedication to deprived children prevents him from spending all the time he should with his own son. However, he resolves the dilemma by deciding that his duty lies in helping the child in most need.

Deprived children, whether because they are orphans or because their own parents are inadequate, are searching for father and mother figures. Lamy acts as a father to Marc and Alain; 'Clemenceau', the gardener at Terneray, stands as a father to Olaf and even plans to adopt him. Mammy, the wife of Croc-Blanc, acts as a substitute mother to all the boys. Lack of a mother's love is the most traumatic deprivation of all. While waiting for a medical examination at the hospital at Denfert-Rochereau, Alain overhears a conversation between nurses about a boy who had been separated from his foster mother by the Social Services. As a result he has fallen ill. His illness is partly psychosomatic, a '*réaction de désarroi* ' brought on by a lack of love (p. 19). One of the nurses comments that emotional and psychological handicaps are worse than physical ones, and she says of the boy's condition: 'Moi, je crois qu'il vaudrait mieux qu'il boite un peu plus et qu'il sache ce que c'est qu'une mère'(p. 19). Cesbron suggests that frustrated filial affection can be sublimated through veneration of the Virgin Mary. It is part of Roman Catholic devotion to regard Mary as "Mother of God", "Mother of the Church", etc. When Alain gazes on a statue of the Virgin in church he sees her as 'sa maman à lui'(p. 122).

The distribution of mail at Terneray is eagerly awaited by those who have families. Alain and other boys like Olaf, who are in the care of the Assistance publique (Child Welfare Services), feel excluded from the excitement. Who is there to write to them ? Alain receives a weekly magazine from Paris and fondly imagines that it is sent by his lost parents who are trying to get in contact with him. When he is suddenly summoned one Sunday to greet a mysterious couple he imagines it is his real parents who have returned to claim him, and his disappointment cannot be contained when he discovers it is the Deroux couple instead. On Sundays the orphans become hypersensitive and cling to the staff, who find themselves caught between immature parents and insecure children. 'Les gars de l'Assistance', writes Cesbron, 'les sans-visites retrouvaient le visage clos et le puits de solitude du jour de leur arrivée'(p. 127). When Olaf is left alone one Sunday, first by Clemenceau and then by Alain, he is desolate. A kind of apartheid is created between those who have parents and those who do not. The former, who are looked after by l'Assistance publique, are nicknamed 'les A.P.' They stick together in the face of the taunts and jibes of the other children, whose ringleader is Pierre Merlerin. A scrap ensues between the two groups with insults being hurled back and forth. Merlerin calls Alain's father 'un minable, un plein de poux, un traîne-savate!'(p. 156) He tells the APs that they were only fostered for money and that Alain's parents abandoned him 'comme une ordure, dans une poubelle'(p. 156). Children can often be cruel to each other, even if they come from stable and happy families. The propensity to thoughtless cruelty is even stronger in children to whom not much love has been given in the first place. As Croc-Blanc says of Alain: 'On ne peut donner que ce qu'on a reçu. Cela fait partie de la justice du monde, de l'horrible logique du monde. Le petit Alain Robert n'a rien à donner'(p. 283).

A Study of delinquency

The novel contains a vivid description of socially deprived children who risk becoming delinquents and slipping into a life of crime. Marc has grown up with a distrustful attitude towards the police. His father is a drunkard and his mother a prostitute. Pierre Merlerin is a violent bully, 'une brute pour qui les autres ne sont que des instruments'(p. 148). He manipulates other, younger children. Aged fifteen, he is a couple of years older than Marc. He is full of pent-up anger against the police, the Palais de Justice, the well-off with their 'appartements de onze pièces', people with flashy American cars and those who have two square meals a day (p. 54). He derives pleasure in taking out his anger and resentment on Darrier. Merlerin's delinquency is rooted in envy towards the better off in a consumer society built on inequalities of wealth and opportunity.

However, the single most important factor in starting a child on the path of delinquency and petty crime is peer pressure.When Merlerin first appears, we see him inducting Marc into the gang and making the younger boy swear an oath of loyalty. It is this same loyalty he calls upon to involve Marc in the escape engineered by Paulo and others. Paulo is a very hard case and Croc-Blanc has all but despaired of him. He steals a five hundred franc note from one of the other boys and only gives himself up after being put under intense moral pressure. Croc-Blanc predicts that he will go from home to home, from institution to institution; when he is let loose on society at the age of twenty-one 'il retrouvera sa famille, ses copains d'enfance: il boira, il volera, comme eux, il se fera pincer'(p. 112). Paulo is a typical example of an adolescent who wants to identify with others of his own

21

background. In order to escape, he knocks out one of the *éducateurs* (Robert) and steals the car of another (Buffalo). His intention is to join up with the Le Havre gang of which he is a member. At the end of the novel he is sent to a borstal and Croc-Blanc's worst fears come true.

The social and environmental causes of delinquency are discussed by Lamy and others. In Marc's locality there are fifteen boys, aged from fifteen to seventeen, working beyond their strength, worn out with fatigue; others are unemployed; some like Marc are still at school and wandering the streets. On the way to Merlerin's home, Darrier comes across scenes of family conflict. Mothers are shouting at their children; he sees a woman being beaten up by her drunken husband, '[une] femme humiliée, sans âge'(p. 51). There are children fighting in the street and, when he tries to separate them, they reply sarcastically: 'Mais, m'sieur, puisqu'on joue au divorce!'(p. 52) The availability of cheap wine and spirits has always made alcoholism a major problem in France (witness Marc's father), and many children were—and still are—exposed to alcohol at an early age. But many home distillers survived the vigorous government anti-alcohol campaign launched in 1954, and Croc-Blanc bemoans the poor example set to young people by 'nos bistrots, nos bouilleurs de cru'(p. 112). Because of their environment, then, many deprived children, according to Croc-Blanc, are doomed to a life of petty crime. He tells Buffalo that he sometimes goes to 'respirer leur air dans leurs quartiers [...]. Ah! mon petit vieux, à leur place, en arrivant ici, je serais dix fois plus dur! '(p. 148)

The values of children and adolescents are healthy in themselves, even though they may be perverted by gang leaders like Merlerin. In the ethos of the juvenile gang there are all the seeds of goodness: solidarity, loyalty and a sense of justice and honour. The enthusiasm shown by Marc and his friends for the building of a clubhouse provides an example of how group loyalty can be channelled into positive directions. Darrier comes to believe that it is important not to detach Marc from the gang but to work through its leader, despite the fact that Merlerin has distinct delinquent tendencies. But Lamy, though originally wishing to convince the lawyer of this, uses the opportunity provided by the petty crime to have Marc removed from le Caïd's influence. He is certainly a bad influence on Marc, because he involves him in Paulo's scheme to escape from Terneray in a stolen car.

However, Merlerin is not all bad. The bullying, scheming side to his personality hides a tender, caring side too, which Mammy brings out when she asks him to look after her son. The children at Terneray have an acute sense of honour. They disapprove of the fact that Paulo has stolen from one of their number but they say nothing to Croc-Blanc or the other members of staff. To inform would be dishonourable. When a boys' court of honour, appointed by Croc-Blanc, meets to judge Marc for the misdemeanor of escaping in a stolen vehicle, it is unable to decide on a suitable sanction. They leave it up to Marc, who deals himself a harsh punishment immediately tempered by Croc-Blanc. Even Paulo has a sense of honour. At first he tries to implicate the others in the assault and theft, even though he knows that he was mainly responsible. But when Lamy appeals to his honour and asks him not to be a false friend to the others he agrees to shoulder the blame.

Doublet accuses young offenders of taking pride in their deviant behaviour and of playing up to an image of themselves as rebels against society. He takes a fatalistic view of delinquency and concedes Lamy's point that the effect of borstal may be counterproductive because offenders are immersed in a criminal environment (p. 236). But he sees no alternative if society is to crack down on delinquency. Instead of reintegration in society, he prescribes banishment through incarceration. He adopts the point of view of the police and supports a stern interpretation of the law. The young should be made to feel intimidated by the solemnity of the Court and by the regalia of the Magistrates. The rituals of the legal process act as deterrents in themselves, as is illustrated when Alain appears before Lamy and Doublet in court. Doublet is described as 'immobile et le regard fixe, tel un oiseau de nuit '(p. 249). He behaves with impatience and condescension towards Alain, whom he considers to be an 'idiot' (pp. 249 and 251). The whole proceedings fill the boy with a feeling of nausea. Doublet wants to commit him to borstal as a punishment for escaping from Terneray. He is more concerned with the misdeed than with the reason behind it. He believes in 'la Progression des Peines'—in other words that each additional offence should automatically carry a stiffer punishment, regardless of mitigating factors (p. 247). In order to be as fair as possible to Doublet's position, Cesbron concedes that there are pitfalls in a naïve and soft approach to delinquents. Merlerin, for example, manipulates doctors, social workers and others. Thus he tries to calculate which approach is most likely to hoodwink Vémard. 'Il se composait un visage à la fois docile et fière, capable de *rassurer* n'importe quel éducateur: "Je l'aurai comme les autres!", pensait-il'(p. 306). In fact he does not succeed, for Vémard is an experienced hand when it comes to dealing with boys like this !

Children in need: a personal and social challenge

The main obstacle to the needs of deprived children is the indifference of society, embodied in the complacency of the bourgeoisie. Doublet preserves his youthful appearance thanks to his 'bonne conscience, ses habitudes régulières, ses certitudes'(p. 131). He takes a pessimistic view of the prospects of children in care. He tends to label them all as potential delinquents and wants a borstal regime to be introduced at Terneray (p. 141). By making them grow up with low expectations and low self-esteem he is imposing a further psychological handicap on them. Doublet represents society's privileged. He is unwilling to empathise with the day-to-day problems experienced by deprived children and their families. According to Lamy, this attitude is typical of the bourgeoisie. Civil servants, bistrot owners, bankers and business men have always been self-satisfied because: ' Eh bien, ils étaient "installés"; et le reste du monde se trouvaient de l'autre côté; *du mauvais côté du comptoir*....'(p. 238). Their consciences are imprisoned behind a wall of indifference and self-satisfaction. The most scathing remarks about society in the novel are made by Tomawak after breaking up the fight between the APs and the others. Tomawak is a communist, or at least a fellow traveller; we can infer this from the newspaper he reads, *Humanité-dimanche* . He despises the exploitatory nature of French and Western society generally. The bourgeoisie adopt a divide and rule policy towards the poor and the working class, setting workers at each others' throats: 'C'est ça, le monde: partout, le pauvre écrasant le pauvre sous le regard des autres qui viennent recruter leurs domestiques!'(pp. 160-161) The class division of society is also attacked by the non-communist Lamy. He condemns the mentality of magistrates who give the impression of walking on the pavement while others walk in the road (p. 134). Bourgeois selfishness and indifference are not uncommon among Christians, as illustrated by the refusal of a Catholic parents' association in the district of Les Carrières to let Marc and his friends build a clubhouse on church-owned land (p. 56).

Cesbron offers two partially overlapping responses to society's selfishness. The first is to call for a personal act of solidarity with the poor and weak in society. Religious faith is one source of inspiration. The other lies in a dispassionate analysis of how well society cares for children in need and in an examination of what needs to be done to prepare them for the adult world. On the personal level, Cesbron emphasises the role of Christian faith and commitment. Religious imagery and allusions abound. Darrier receives blows from Merlerin as an act of atonement. 'Il est en train,' writes Cesbron, 'de *racheter* chacun des gosses au grand Caïd' and he believes that one good act can save the world (p. 54). Lamy, too, is convinced that the merits of the good man can compensate for the weakness of others. 'En ce moment même, peut-être, à cause de mon désespoir à moi, un appel mystérieux serre le cœur d'un jeune homme...'(p. 314) Implied in these statements is Cesbron's belief in the Communion of Saints and in the Roman Catholic theology of redemption, which holds that the Christian shares in Christ's redeeming work. Other religious allusions are to be found. Mammy shows trust in Merlerin because she is inspired by the parable of the lost sheep. When Croc-Blanc hesitates to have Alain as godfather to his son, Lamy appeals to his conscience, reminding him that the Christian must have a faith strong enough to overcome the cynicism of the world. Croc-Blanc stresses the importance of the example set by individual Christians in the Social Services who give 'plus qu'ils ne reçoivent'(p. 305). Of all the characters, Lamy represents the most powerful voice of the Christian conscience, and the power of his faith and goodness is witnessed by the change of heart he brings about in Doublet. He wants a spiritual conversion of the whole legal profession that will bear fruit in a greater emphasis on re-education and a lesser on punishment. He believes that Juvenile Magistrates should take the initiative in putting compassion first and set an example to the ordinary courts. Lamy's declamatory monologues give him the aura of a religious prophet. From his office window he looks out upon the Sainte-Chapelle in the heart of the Palais de Justice and describes it as a symbol of Christ ensnared by the legal apparatus of the State, 'prisonnière parmi nos pierres noires, nos archives rancunières'(p. 239).

The predominance of working-class children in care and the failure of society to tackle the problem of social inequality that results from class divisions are evoked by Vémard. He wants to give young working-class offenders a sense of pride in their own class and to equip them to survive in a capitalist society through self-reliance and skill in a trade. The centre he runs is called "La Main Tendue", a politically as well as a socially significant title because it was the very phrase used by the French Communist Party in the mid-1930s to characterise its conciliatory policy towards Catholics. By the time *Chiens perdus sans collier* was written, all hope of dialogue and rapprochement between the Communist Party and the Church had vanished under the impact of the Cold War. Indeed the Catholic Croc-Blanc, with whom Vémard enters into debate, asks why the Church is persecuted in communist countries. Vémard does not rise to the bait. Notwithstanding the ideological and religious differences between the two men, a large area of consensus emerges on the right approach to take to socially deprived children. Real cooperation on the ground is possible between professionals who are committed to the welfare of young people, regardless of other differences that may divide them. Vémard attacks the bourgeois ethos of the traditional children's home, which cuts children off from their working-class backgrounds. Croc-Blanc concedes that he has a point, although he reminds Vémard that at least children are taught a trade. Vémard retorts that children's homes are responsible for inculcating low self-esteem because of their paternalism and appeal to Christian charity. '"Un œil sur les gosses et un œil au ciel", c'est la définition du vieux Baden-Powell, votre maître', he says (p. 300). Working-class children need working-class adults to encourage and guide them. Vémard implicitly criticises the social gulf between the middle-class doctors, lawyers and social workers who deal in a professional capacity with working-class children. An example of this is seen in the difficulty Darrier experiences in gaining the confidence of Marc's gang. Vémard attacks social workers for behaving like policemen or snoops (Darrier), doctors for being fatalistic

26

(Clérant), *éducateurs* for being over-optimistic (Mammy), and magistrates for being paternalistic (Lamy). There is a danger, according to Vémard, of the child being surrounded by specialists who submit him to a battery of medical and psychiatric tests. In such circumstances, the child may come to consider himself as a "problem case" and not as a person to be taken seriously. There is a danger that he will be reduced to the level of 'un chien perdu sans collier'(p. 303).

Structure, style and characterisation

At one level the story revolves around the experiences of two boys from similar deprived backgrounds. At another level there is a continuous stream of comment on the nature of the social, moral and religious questions posed by deprivation and delinquency. The novel highlights the role of various groups involved in child welfare and underlines the class structure of society. We are given a glimpse into different worlds: those of the children themselves, doctors, Juvenile Magistrates, the police, journalists and staff in the children's home. The story is told through the eyes of an omniscient author, who even intervenes directly in the story to comment on the nature of the problems being explored. The novel can be characterised as sentimental, conventional and full of dramatic incident: for example, the appearance of the police at the club house-warming party in search of Marc, the chance meeting between Lamy and Alain shortly after the latter's second escape from the home, and the final courtroom scene. In many respects the novel brings to mind the melodramatic structure of the nineteenth-century novel. It is full of changes of scene: Lamy's home and office, the Palais de Justice, the hospital at Denfert-Rochereau, the slum district of Les Carrières and, in contrast to the city, the countryside around Terneray. The plot unfolds chronologically with no flashbacks. Dialogue and descriptive passages are interspersed with long monologues which serve to articulate different aspects of the problem of deprivation and delinquency. However, the monologues (mainly delivered by Lamy) are somewhat stilted and over-rhetorical in style and tend to slow down the pace of the story. The author intervenes twice to pass moral judgment (pp. 193 and 269). He

27

conducts an imaginary dialogue with his readers:

> Ce n'est pas notre faute, s'il y a des enfants et des chiens perdus! et des filles enceintes qui se noient! et des pères qui tuent leur gosse à coups de talon! Ce n'est pas notre faute s'il y a des taudis, des bistrots, du chômage, et des gosses qui volent et qui se prostituent!
>
> —Alors, si ce n'est *pas du tout* votre faute, pourquoi le criez-vous si fort ? Si vous êtes *tout à fait* innocents, pourquoi cela vous empêche-t-il de dormir ? Si vous ne pouvez *absolument rien* pour cet enfant sauvage et ce chien martyr, pour tous ces enfants perdus qui ne sont pas les vôtres, pouquoi n'avez-vous pas déjà fermé ce livre ? (p. 193)

These lines are characteristic of Cesbron's style. The common fate ascribed to children and stray dogs refers back to the novel's title. Cesbron uses the possessive adjective 'notre' to suggest that he and his readers try to salve their consciences by putting the blame for child deprivation on to others. The tone in the first paragraph, punctuated by exclamation marks, is one of shrill sarcasm. Typically, he employs highly emotive, even sensationalist language to evoke the brutality and resulting despair to which society's weak fall victim. The abrupt change to 'vous' in the second paragraph signals a more direct attack on the reader's conscience. By distancing himself from the reader, Cesbron assumes the objective voice of conscience. In order to convey moral earnestness, he puts italicized stress on certain words. The passage employs a number of rhetorical devices to challenge the reader's conscience: phrases and words are repeated, images of violence and deprivation are accumulated, and direct questions are fired in quick succession. The tone is forced and the stylistic mannerisms somewhat hackneyed, but at least no punches are pulled in order to shake the reader out of his complacency.

Cesbron tends to preach a message and the novel falls into the category of the *roman à thèse* . All those involved in child welfare are described as devoted professionals, struggling against public indifference and a slow-moving bureaucracy. The children are portrayed as three-dimensional characters with strengths, weaknesses, fears and hopes. Their use of nicknames (*Croc-Blanc* , *Ballon-Captif* , *Radar* , *Velours* , *Taka* , etc.) is typical of the linguistic inventiveness of children of their age. They also have vivid imaginations and indulge in make-believe: for example, the web of fantasy that Alain weaves around the Palais de Justice (p. 5). The adult characters are less convincing because they tend to be oversimplified. They are made to voice the cause of child welfare and their words and actions are designed to suggest moral strength and integrity. Doublet acts as a counterpoint, embodying selfishness and lack of compassion. In a manner reminiscent of Balzacian characterisation, physical features are used to underline a character's moral qualities. Thus Doublet is described disparagingly as having 'un visage qui ne vieillirait pas, préservé par sa bonne conscience, ses habitudes régulières, ses certitudes'(p. 131). Darrier's features, on the other hand, are more kindly drawn: 'Jeune, un peu voûté [...] un sourire voltarien entre des rides profondes' which prompts Lamy to observe: "'C'est injuste: *il vieillit pour les autres ...*'"(pp. 40 and 41)

Words like 'Vie' and 'Espoir', written with capital letters, are used allegorically at the end of the novel to exemplify the spirit of childhood. Birds are used to symbolise liberty (p. 181). The author waxes lyrical in his description of the changing seasons in the countryside. The language of officialdom is used pejoratively, notably in the first chapter, with the repetition of the word *dossier* (also written with a capital letter). It is also sometimes underlined in the text and is accompanied by other related words: *papelards* , *tampons* , *rapports* , *feuillets de tous formats* . By contrast, religious imagery, which runs as a leitmotif throughout the novel, is used to express the author's own Catholic faith. At one point Alain confuses 'Je vous salue Marie' with 'Sainte Mammy, mère de Dieu'(p. 216). Whether this is an example of the author expressing piety, making a clever pun or being mawkish is a matter of taste and opinion.

In *Chiens perdus sans collier* , Cesbron presents a forceful analysis of the issues involved in child deprivation but fails to capture the ambiguity of people and situations. By writing a sort of fictional journalism his polemical intent has, according to some critics, detracted from the aesthetic appeal of his novels. Thus Bertrand Poirot-Delpech, writing in *Le Monde* of 14 August 1979, makes the point that: 'Cette exigence fait passer le cas de conscience avant l'effet de l'art.' However, it could be argued that the novel's unsophisticated style is appropriate to subject matter which does not call for literary artifice and psychological subtlety. After all, the needs of deprived children are simple and straightforward and society's obligations towards them glaringly obvious.

NOTES

(1) Monique Detry, *Profil perdu. Un Autre Regard sur l'œuvre de Cesbron* (Paris, 1978), p. 81.

(2) Theodore Zeldin, *France 1848-1945, Vol. II : Intellect, Taste and Anxiety* (Oxford, 1977), pp. 914-5. (Gives useful summary of statistics relating to juvenile crime in nineteenth-century France).

(3) Alphonse Daudet, *Jack* (Paris, 1973), pp. 417-21.

(4) Comité d'études sur la violence, la criminalité et la délinquance, *Réponses à la violence. Rapport du comité d'études sur la violence, la criminalité et la délinquance, présidé par Alain Peyrefitte* , Tome 2 (Paris, 1977), p. 241.

(5) W.E. Vaz, 'Juvenile Gang Delinquency in Paris', in *Juvenile Delinquency. A Book of Readings* , ed. Rose Giallombardo (New York, 1966), pp. 309-318.

(6) M.Fry, M.Grünhat, H. Mannheim, W.Grabinska, *Lawless Youth : A Challenge to the new Europe* (London, 1947), p. 180.

(7) Barbara Wooten, 'A Social Scientist's Approach to Maternal Deprivation', in *Deprivation of Maternal Care: A Reassessment of its Effects* (Geneva, 1962), p. 72.

La Clé sur la porte

Marie Cardinal: life and work

In 1962, Marie Cardinal won an international book prize for her work *Ecoutez la mer* . From the start she has considered herself a feminist writer who has tried to show the different struggles of women, young and old. In *La Mule du corbillard* (1964), a retiring old lady harbours a deep hatred for the man who dispossessed her of her property. Her intense love of her land goes hand in hand with a strong desire for vengeance. In *La Souricière* (1965), a young mother locked in fear, self-loathing and hatred of others seeks a way out of her unhappiness through a love affair. Cardinal's political commitment and feminist activities led her to record the thoughts of Gisèle Halimi in *La Cause des femmes* (1973). In 1967, she brought out a very candid autobiography entitled *Cet été-là* . But the most moving novel, for which she received the Prix Littré, was *Les Mots pour le dire* (1976). It is the story of her life, her nervous breakdown bordering on madness and recourse to psychoanalysis. In 1976, in collaboration with Annie Leclerc, she wrote a sequel to this work, entitled *Autrement dit* . She always longed one day to return to Algeria and to Algiers where she was born, and in *Au pays de mes racines* (1980) she records the moving journey to the land of her birth. It is a work full of affectionate nostalgia for her country and its past. Her latest novel, *Les Grands désordres* (1987), is about a mother and her drug-addict daughter. *La Clé sur la porte* , published in 1971, was made into a film in 1978 and directed by Yves Boisset.

Cardinal comes from a family of French Algerian colonialists, proud of their traditions. She can trace her roots back to 1837 when a young aristocrat from Bordeaux, a marquis, went with his mistress (a married woman) to Algeria. He was the founder of the vineyards which kept her family until 1962. Her own father was an engineer who was gassed in the First World War and sent by the army in 1918 to Algeria. There he met her

31

mother and they married. The marriage was not a happy one, and they separated in 1929, the year Cardinal was born. Her mother was embittered by the experience and nursed a lifelong resentment against her husband.

In her writings she describes the typical French colonialist as a father figure, lord and boss who enjoyed quasi-feudal rights over the natives. It was this very paternalism and lack of political consciousness which led to the army-led insurrection against the granting of Algerian independence. Cardinal's own life has been scarred by the Algerian war. In 1953 she married a French Algerian who belonged to the same Catholic, upper-middle-class milieu as she did. They have three children. When she left Algeria after the birth of her second child, she little realised that she would never return. She dreamt of revisiting Algiers, which she associated with hot, sunny weather, far removed from the cold climate and social stuffiness of France. However, she was reluctant to go back for fear of being overwhelmed by sadness at the disappearance of her family roots and by nostalgia for a lost past.

On leaving Algeria, Cardinal joined her husband in France, where he had obtained his *agrégation* (the highest teaching diploma). They lived abroad for a number of years. She taught during this period. After her mother died she resolved to make a psychological and moral break with her Algerian past. There is a great difference between the woman she was and the woman she became. She spent seven years undergoing psychoanalysis three times a week, seeking to overcome a neurosis partly brought on by her rigid and repressive upbringing. She had to free herself from caste and class which, out of love and respect for her mother, she had never judged. Because of the strain put upon her marriage by her condition, her husband left to work in Canada, leaving her and the children in France. There was no divorce, and she and the children would join him every summer. They were 'un vrai couple mais un couple subversif', who had rejected bourgeois conformism.[1] When *Autrement dit* was published, they had already been married over twenty-three years and their marriage had survived long periods of separation. With her husband in Canada, however, she effectively became a single parent for most of the year, with responsibility for bringing up three children. Her illness prevented her from taking up a teaching career. She supported her family by doing part-time jobs such as

32

secretarial work, proofreading, journalism and any work that she could do at home. This lasted for sixteen years, during which time she also wrote and had published a number of works. Nevertheless it was a time of considerable hardship—social security benefits were only paid to writers in France from January 1977.

Apart from the mental and emotional conflict involved in her effort to break free from the outlook instilled in her from childhood, she suffered a deeper psychic pain: the knowledge that her mother had never wanted her to be born and had even contemplated having an abortion. She found that writing was one way of releasing repressed emotions. *La Clé sur la porte* ends with a prose poem written by one of her children's friends, a girl named Moussia, who has discovered that her mother had wanted to abort her. Writing acts as a form of catharsis. For Cardinal, coming to terms with the knowledge that she was an unwanted child led to a mental breakdown later in life, and it was only thanks to psychoanalysis and to her children that her mental health was restored. Her cure coincided with the onset of her children's adolescence, and she wanted to avoid at all costs inflicting on them the suffocating conformity and moral hypocrisy she had endured from her own mother. She tried to impress on them the importance of always being true to oneself and of looking critically at social norms and conventions. This involves risks, but equally there are risks in not living authentically. Family life should be built on self-respect and respect for others. She was also indebted to her children for widening her taste in music and books. She wanted to achieve a depth and quality of communication with them that was lacking in her relationship with her own mother. The emotional cost, she records, was very high and, looking back on her life, she is amazed she held up. It was an exhausting and frequently frustrating time, but eventually she and her children got to know and respect each other. She had to answer a battery of questions, some banal, some philosophical. She tried to be as patient as possible with her children so that they might learn through personal experience that dirtiness and laziness grow out of maladjustment and moral malaise and lead to unhappiness. As a result, her children became more self-aware and more sensitive to other people. Although there were frayed tempers and tantrums, harmony was restored and her life with her children became very happy. In order to understand them more fully, she kept the key in the door and welcomed their friends into the flat. She writes: 'A cette époque, j'ai vu passer des centaines de jeunes.' [2] Those who kept coming back had emotional and psychological problems which stemmed, without exception, from their relationships with their mothers. She discovered that the love between mother and child is built on understanding, but also that it falters due to generational incomprehension. She concludes that it is hard being a mother today. There is so much work, fatigue, loneliness and self-denial to be endured.

In *La Clé sur la porte* , Cardinal assumes the unpolemical voice of a concerned mother. However, she is also very alive to the way French society discriminates against mothers and women in general and, in her essays and autobiographical works, she adopts a more pointedly feminist stance. She attacks the way the image of motherhood has been abused by the State (*mère-patrie*) and by politicians and advertisers. A lapsed Catholic herself, she is especially critical of the Church for holding up in the figure of the Virgin Mary an ideal of womanhood which seems to devalue the lives of ordinary women. She describes the influence of the Church on her own mother as corrosive, because it prevented her from understanding herself, and thereby constituted a barrier to communication with her own daughter. The laws of the Catholic Church, she argues, combine male power and feline deviousness; these are used to manipulate women by extolling self-sacrifice and bourgeois morality. Power is wielded in society by men, who have turned women into objects, and women have only the power to lie, to *ruser* .

For Cardinal, writing is a way of rebelling against male domination and of articulating how ordinary women feel. She hopes that readers will recognize in her a Frenchwoman of today 'qui ressemble, dans le fond, à toutes les femmes.' [3] Women's wisdom, she writes, is intuitive and grows out of their intimate relationship with their husbands and children. As one critic has put it, Marie Cardinal 'vise à déconstruire ce qu'il y a de masculin dans l'écriture, les structures du logos, pour donner la parole au corps féminin.' [4] As a child, she received from her family and school all the knowledge, vocabulary and signs which enabled her to identify with and benefit from society. However, she had never been encouraged to think as a woman, and this became a factor in her later neurosis.

Cardinal is curiously silent about the effect on her of being fatherless. Her childhood and adolescence were conditioned by an intense and emotionally fraught relationship with her mother, who gave her a very negative impression of her own father and, implicitly, of fatherhood in general.The absence of a father had the effect of making the mother-daughter relationship more claustrophobic than it might otherwise have been and was, at least in her own case, a factor contributory to the neurosis that developed in her adulthood. Her treatment of the family in *La Clé sur la porte* is written from the perspective of a single mother, and it is difficult to glean from this very autobiographical story what influence her (admittedly absent) husband has on the children.

A Portrait of middle-class youth

With the postwar demographic boom was born in France a new cult of youth and motherhood. In the late 1960s there were twice as many people under the age of twenty-five as in 1939, although the overall population had only risen by 25%.[5] Whereas young people were once ignored, now they became a focus of attention for the media, politicians and the advertising industry. 'La jeunesse' became the symbol of a dynamic and modern France. Traditionally, young people were seen as timid and conformist. A report of 1966 concluded: 'Ils ne pensent que par rapport à eux-mêmes et rares sont ceux qui pensent à se réunir pour une action généralisée.' [6]

In May 1968, students in Paris took to the streets to protest against the state of the French University, although the demonstrations quickly turned into a more general protest against consumer society. The docile image of youth seemed to be overturned. But after the initial upsurge of militancy there was a return to normality. The militants were only a minority, and the vast majority remained an enigma. When Gaullist authority was reasserted, the students were disorientated and did not know what to think. Yet May '68 made both adults and young people look more critically at French society, and both the mother in the story, Marie, and her children are affected by the events. Marie would have been around forty in 1968, and therefore too old to be a student demonstrator. The formative political influence on her own generation was the Algerian war. However, she lives the events of May vicariously through her own children and draws from them encouragement to pursue her own personal emancipation from bourgeois society. It is notable that it is she , and not her children, who is keen to see *lycéens* stepping up militant action at the beginning of the school year (p. 145). The novel is set in 1971-72, and her eldest child would only have been fifteen in 1968. In other words, her children would have been too young to be active participants, although they saw the utopian dreams of 1968 evaporate. As a result they have become disillusioned with revolutionary politics. Marie and her children are now vaguely left-wing, or *gauchiste* , and despise the authoritarianism of the communists. Charlotte says of them: 'Les cocos, c'est pire que les bourgeois '(p. 158).

One of the concrete outcomes of May was a re-evaluation of the French educational system. The problem of the French school was that it provided little human contact. The new Minister of Education, Edgar Faure, wanted to open up a new dialogue between pupils and teachers, and schools' councils were set up which included parents, pupils, teachers, Ministry officials and local dignitaries. In the aftermath of '68 the school became a battleground, with parents and others who wanted traditional pedagogy and discipline on one side and supporters of a more liberal regime in schools on the other. Marie takes a disparaging line towards the first group, whom she dismisses as 'des imbéciles'(p. 48).

Marie wants to create an environment for herself, her children and their friends in which there is love and communication. In her concern for what is authentic in life she reflects an existentialist outlook that has loomed large in postwar French culture. She strives to impress on her children that it is more important to be than to have. She wants her children to grow up as individuals and to develop their faculties to the fullest extent. The problem is how to enable a young person to develop his or her own individuality without losing a sense of social discipline. Marie's decision to allow her children to invite home all their friends and acquaintances brings this dilemma into sharp focus.

The French social scientist Raymond Aron has made a disparaging assessment of the events of May '68, and to the question: "who is rejecting society ?" he has replied that it is middle-class youth, brought up by overindulgent or uninterested parents.[7] The young have had material comforts too easily, he argues, and would arrogantly deny them to the less privileged. They rebel against consumer society and, when that fails, become dropouts. They lack the incentive to succeed and are too ready to judge society. They illustrate the phenomenon which the French sociologist, Emile Durkheim, has defined as *anomie* , namely a condition of aimlessness and listlessness brought on by alienation from society. Most of the young people in the novel display "anomic" behaviour. In its severest form it can lead to suicide, drug addiction (Lakdar and others), or the cult of *débilité* (which will be examined later). Many bemused parents, like those of the Clamarts, are drawn into supporting their dropout sons and daughters. Marie is afraid this will happen in the case of her own children. However, the young middle-class American *paumés* who stay in the flat are so pathetic and crass that they unwittingly serve Marie's purpose of dissuading her children from imitating them. It is significant that *anomie* is a particular characteristic of middle-class youth, because the material prosperity of an advanced industrial society like France can support a large, alienated sub-culture, and also very typical of Marie that she should argue for a non-Marxian interpretation of the verb *aliéner* with Jean-François, the "philosopher" of the Daltons.

As a middle-class parent, the author is well placed to analyse the failures and mistakes of other parents like herself. Some cling obsessively to their children and make them conform against their wishes to the family's expectations of them. Sarah's parents, for example, do not treat her as a young adult, nor do they try to understand why she wants to be an artist. Parents hold on to family traditions because they feel insecure, thus making it more difficult for their children to trust and confide in them. Marie's flat provides a haven for many children of such parents. When they become morose and listless in adolescence, their parents panic. The family unit is becoming more unstable, parents are no longer sure of their role, and the French school does not assume responsibility for developing pupils' characters. Alienation from the Church, which was prevalent among the French working class in the nineteenth century, is now spreading among the middle class. The family is in crisis at every level of society, and there is an

37

increasing incidence of drug addiction and suicides. Cardinal stresses again and again that the key to family breakdown is lack of communication and love between parents and children. If *La Clé sur la porte* has a message—and it is not a didactic novel—it is this.

One of the main characteristics of young people in France and throughout Western society is their attachment to individual freedom. They regard it as very important to be able to dispose of their own time as they please and to feel that they are in command of their own lives. This is true of adults too, who have to find a compromise between their desire for leisure on the one hand and job and family commitments on the other. In the case of young people, parents and school are often seen as the main obstacles to the attainment of freedom and self-expression. Individual freedom, one study concludes, is seen as so important that 'les jeunes en ont fait une règle de vie.' [8] They want to squeeze the maximum out of the present. Leisure takes priority over time spent productively. Marie, for example, notes how long adolescents spend daydreaming (p. 33). The danger is that too much individualism can weaken social involvement and hamper understanding between the generations. The jargon of young people constitutes an added hindrance to communication between them and their parents and teachers. It also makes it more difficult for them to conceptualise or describe complex realities. Bertrand, for example, uses *débile* to describe virtually everything, and Marie comments drily: 'Heureusement que le mot "débile" existe, sinon je me demande comment il s'exprimerait'(p. 77). Young people want to avoid being caught in the web of consumer society, but at the same time they want to feel they have a stake in society. However, obtaining diplomas no longer guarantees a secure job. In the late 1960s and early '70s there were already not enough jobs available in France for the numbers of arts students graduating. Nevertheless, unemployment of graduates was not as acute then as it has become in the 1980s.

The young people Cardinal describes are not very interested in politics. This is ironic, given that the events of May were very recent history. No doubt this can be ascribed to disillusionment that nothing changed, but there are other reasons too for their political apathy. The power of the media shapes social attitudes, and the role of the advertising industry creates needs. School subjects like history and economics tend to be taught from the same perspective, and a radical questioning of accepted wisdom is discouraged. The decline of political consciousness in modern youth is also to be explained by the fact that they did not live through periods of major struggle like the mid-1930s (the Popular Front government and the rise of Fascism) or the Resistance, compared to which May '68 was small beer. They have lost all sense of patriotism, regarding France as only a politico-administrative infrastructure. Their vision is no longer national but European, and even global. Since there exists a world-wide youth culture it is difficult for young people to have a sense of their own national and cultural roots. They find it difficult to identify their aspirations with the policies of organised political parties and to become involved in local or national politics. Their enthusiasm and commitment is focussed on their own group or on some world issue like famine or human rights. Finally, it is worth noting that the youth culture Cardinal portrays is part of an urban sub-culture. Rural France, which remains attached to traditional peasant values, is alien to the young people depicted. Young people in France are concentrated in big cities, and it is there that they evolve their values and life styles.

Rejection of bourgeois values

The word "bourgeois" is used by Cardinal in a specific sense to denote old-established families like her own in which family wealth and position are inherited from one generation to the next, and in which there is a strict social code of behaviour. The term harks back to the nineteenth century. "Classes moyennes" is a twentieth-century term denoting white-collar salaried workers who do not live on inherited wealth. However, there is considerable social overlap between both groups, whose values are described pejoratively as "bourgeois". Marie's adult life has been one of gradual emancipation from the values of the bourgeoisie. Her whole life has been affected by her upper middle-class, Catholic and colonialist upbringing. The education she received may have equipped her to take her place in middle-class society, but it failed to fulfil her as a person. Her children are the children of middle-class parents. She wonders how they can break free from bourgeois conformity without becoming trendy radicals or naïve philanthropists. She describes the typical bourgeois family as a straitjacket 'qui pèse lourd, qui blesse les jeunes et les adultes'(p. 41). She describes the traditional family as an enclosed space where human beings are like flies continually bumping into each other. It seems to Marie that the prewar model of the family is out of date, and that the stereotyped view of family life it has fostered is an anachronism and a trap.

Marie's mother is the person who has the dominant influence upon her and who, ironically, is the source and inspiration of her rebellious spirit. Her mother weaves in and out of the story, providing a counterpoint to Marie's own experience of motherhood. The visit to the family graveyard is used to symbolise the failure of the bourgeoisie to adopt a wholesome attitude to life. Marie's mother would stop at paupers' graves and say: 'Ils sont mieux là qu'ailleurs', implying that it is better to be dead than poor (p. 43). Marie records that she was always filled with dread whenever a member of the family said: 'Si ça continue nous irons mendier dans la rue'(p. 43). In the bourgeois order of things, wealth divided the poor from the rich in death as well as in life. The mortal remains of those whose families could not pay for their graves in perpetuity were transferred to an ossuary. Marie reflects sarcastically that, just as the poor lived in overcrowded tenement buildings in life, so in death it was natural for their bones to be piled up in charnel-houses. In contrast, the wealthy, who could afford to own villas, were able to have proper graves, 'chaque famille bien séparée de ses voisines. C'était logique'(p. 45).

Her relationship with her mother was based on a rigid code of behaviour. Her sarcastic catalogue of the clichés by which her mother made her live is reminiscent of Gustave Flaubert's survey of the *idées reçues* of the bourgeoisie contained in *Bouvard et Pécuchet*.. She had to learn the minutiae of table manners, and she concludes that from all this brainwashing nothing much is left except 'manger proprement et être courtois'(p. 92).

Her mother's family embodied the nationalist and colonialist values that were typical of their class. She describes a party for the workers organised by her family on her grandmother's estate in Algeria; significantly, a young grape harvester dies, practically before her eyes, of malnutrition and heat exhaustion (pp. 137-40). Her mother, who used the occasion to dispense charity, regarded wealth as a blessing from God for a virtuous life. Material comfort was a stamp of moral superiority. One could not, according to Marie's mother, be a respectable person if one lived in a slum, if one did not know the right people, and if one had not been taught proper etiquette. The poor were responsible for their poverty because they were lazy at school and lived on top of each other. Her mother's charitable endeavours were directed not at the poor Europeans, but at the Arabs. They are described through the mother's eyes as a 'race oubliée du monde, abandonnée de Dieu'(p. 135). Not only were they poor and of another race, but they were of another religion too. The Catholic Church, with its white, European roots, is portrayed as abetting such complacent colonialism and racialism. Her mother considers the task of helping Arabs especially difficult, because they are not Catholics and one cannot speak to them of the Virgin Mary, Jesus, Joseph, Cain, Abel, St. Francis of Assisi, St. Theresa of Lisieux and St. Bernadette of Lourdes. She wonders, given their 'superstitions risibles' (p. 136), how they can be reached. Frenchmen had to serve as examples, to be saints in order to bring the Arabs to the Christian God.

Marie recalls that by the age of twelve she had had instilled in her the "preordained" hierarchy of the world. First there was God, secondly the rich with, in order of precedence, the aristocracy, the upper followed by the lower middle class and, lower still down the social scale, the traders. Even if they were richer than aristocrats, traders had less status because they did not understand proper etiquette and had no breeding. After the rich came the poor: firstly the poor whites (the French were better than the Spaniards or the Italians). At the bottom of the rung were the Arabs. Her mother would refer to them as a cross to be borne, but Marie remarks acidly : 'Moi, je ne sentais pas le poids de cette croix et j'en avais honte'(p. 137). She describes how her family was able subtly to manipulate the good will of the natives, and how its paternalism masked contempt. Deeply-encrusted colonialist instincts lie dormant even in Marie, and come out unconsciously. Lakdar, the Algerian boy, becomes very insecure and deferential in his manner towards her and, without noticing it, she begins to boss him around. Marie wants to shake off her bourgeois conditioning, to shed the uniform of a

41

'femme bourgeoise-chrétienne-méditerranéenne' and to put behind her 'cet hier qui ne veut pas crever tout à fait'(p. 177).

Marie's revolt against her mother's values is gradual: firstly there is her realisation, when still a girl, that her mother's charity was only possible because of the poverty that arose from social and economic inequalities. By the time she had reached adolescence, Marie describes herself as fun-loving, carefree and already at odds with the social oppressiveness of her milieu. Thus her description of how, during Sunday Mass, she would daydream of being with her boyfriend underlines her desire to escape inwardly from the rituals of Catholic bourgeois conformity. By the time she married, she implies, she had already rejected the Catholicism of her youth. But she still remained a *bourgeoise* at heart. She describes how, in the early years of her marriage, she remained a houseproud wife attached to material possessions. She was part of 'la gauche festive'(p. 89). She would weep over the lot of the Third World while drinking her Black Label whisky. Deep down she saw her children as surgeons and actors of genius, while claiming it would not worry her one jot if they became taxi drivers or plumbers. Her love of material possessions, which was like an umbilical cord tying her to the bourgeoisie, was only broken when her husband's flat in Montreal was burned down. He had a fashionably decorated apartment which she describes sarcastically as 'un cadre à la mode des intellectuels'(p. 95). His friends were similar examples of radical chic and epitomised 'le hippisme de luxe'(p. 96). She argues with her husband, accusing him of hypocrisy. Throughout their seventeen years of marriage he had exhorted her to resist the temptation to conform to middle-class mores. Under his influence she had changed, and now she found her husband's friends superficial. She disapproves of his new life style, which she dubs 'une connerie et un scandale'(p. 98). When a petrol can accidently sets fire to the flat, destroying everything, she regards it as a form of liberation: 'Enfin libre. Enfin séparée de ces foutaises'(p. 102).

However, it is her mother's death which marks the most decisive stage in her emancipation from her bourgeois roots. Marie was thirty-eight at the time. The death of parents, she writes, always represents an opportunity for children to attain a higher degree of moral autonomy and emotional independence. Thanks to her closeness to her own children and their friends, she manages to break free from the mould in which she was cast. She rejects, both in principle and practice, the way she was brought up, and adopts a totally different approach to being a parent . She wants to be near her children 'parce qu'ils m'intéressent, parce que c'est avec eux que ma vie commence'(p. 177). The presence of children has changed her life dramatically. She writes: 'J'ai l'impression de vivre plus et mieux'(p. 11). She is no longer preoccupied by material problems of secondary importance and no longer has a round of social events. Most of her friends no longer call because they are uneasy in the presence of young people. Life in the household is simple. Her children forced her to choose between continuing or rejecting the lifestyle of a smug, middle-class liberal. She has chosen a life which is not comfortably middle-class in any sense of the word.

Her rejection of the bourgeois ethos is personal and not political. She does not prescribe any specific political or economic policies for reforming the system, and she certainly does not call for revolution. However, she spurns those institutions and values which she identifies with her own upbringing. The path she has chosen is one of personal fulfilment and happiness. She does not want to be against anyone, but happy in herself and thereby able, as a mother, to transmit her own inner peace and happiness to her children. It is true of course that Marie and her family lived through the events of May, and that she supported youth's spontaneous protest against bourgeois values and institutions, notably the educational system. However, May '68 was not a revolutionary movement but a mass movement of protest. Marie concludes that to shed the inauthentic values of the bourgeoisie is the task of a lifetime and that old habits can resurface, as seen in her own treatment of Lakdar. Moreover, she is unsure whether the way she has chosen of instilling a sense of freedom and self-respect in her children is the right way, although she retains her faith in her nonconformist philosophy of life.

A study of the generation gap

The novel brings into focus the conflict between the generations: firstly, the conflict between her mother's generation and her own; secondly, despite

43

Marie's efforts to bridge it, the yawning gap between her own generation and her children's. The underlying causes are examined: the breakdown in communication between parents and children, the abandonment of parental responsibility, and the lack of trust and respect between parents and children. The social factors exacerbating the generation gap are also discussed, notably the speed of change within society and the influence of the media on young people. Lastly, the effects of the divide between the generations are described. Parents and grandparents on the one hand, and young people on the other, have different perceptions of the past. The young also have their own music, and this creates a common worldwide bond.

Marie cannot comprehend why her own contemporaries, who reached adolescence after 1945, have experienced a breakdown in communication with their children. She can well understand why those who were adolescents before or during the 1939-1945 war are not on the same wavelength as the young. They had a different upbringing and were moulded by a different historical experience. But parents of her own generation, born after 1945, have a lot in common with their children. The music of the postwar era has influenced contemporary music: boogie-woogie, swing, etc. The idols of her own generation—Juliette Greco, Sartre, Camus and Boris Vian—are still popular with today's youth.

She considers that her own generation was one of transition and that, although they spoke of free love, they remained partially under the thrall of the generation of 1914, for whom valour on the battlefield and patriotism were paramount virtues. However, she doubts whether those of her generation who married between 1952 and 1956 really wanted to raise their children in the cult of the Viennese Waltz, of Joan of Arc and of top-heavy Marianne, the French equivalent of Britannia (p. 35). For this reason she finds it difficult to explain why parents of her own generation fail to understand their own children, who are only bringing to fulfilment what they started. She looks at herself: she is from a divorced family, she had a difficult childhood, she listened to records and read, but enjoyed the sunshine and open air life of the Mediterranean, where communication and openness to others come more easily. Friends of hers who sowed their wild oats or, as Marie puts it, got up to 'dingueries insensées', make no better parents than their parents and grandparents. They want their children off their hands as soon as possible. Children require sacrifices from parents, many of whom have become selfish and materialistic. As the author says: 'le fric pourrit, c'est une vérité première'(p. 36). Children become a form of investment, and in the love parents feel for them there is 'une bonne part d'attendrissement sur soi-même'(p. 36). Parents expect a good return on all the time and money they have spent on their children, who then feel pressurised to pass their *baccalauréat* , become engineers, surgeons, teachers, managers, etc. They are expected to achieve the same standard of living as their parents, but when they reach the age of thirteen they become sullen, play truant, and their parents lose contact with them. To win back their trust and affection, parents lavish money and presents on them. When that fails to work they panic and, losing patience, start to crack down: 'C'est le contrôle constant. C'est la guerre'(p. 37). Most of the children come to the flat because they are not shown enough attention by neglectful parents, who pass on to the school the responsibility of teaching discipline. Marie attends a parents' meeting at Dorothée's school and is appalled to hear parents calling for a return to 'le bon système d'antan', when strict discipline was enforced in schools (p. 47).

Marie surveys the 1950s and 1960s in which her children's generation grew up. There were wars in Algeria, Pakistan, the Middle East and Vietnam, not to mention conflict in Northern Ireland. Racialism became a national and international issue, there was the walk on the moon, the advent of colour television, Concorde, the pill, heart transplants, atomic weapons and guerrilla warfare, while the harsh realities of drugs, pollution, unemployment and injustice were all beamed into the family living room via television. In the light of modern reality, nostalgic memories of the Great War and the Resistance can seem irrelevant. Because modern society has become so complex, simple advice is no longer of much use to children. The world has become *flou* and chaotic. Today it is no longer parents who impart information to children. They get it from television, cinema, cartoons and their peers. Parents are no longer 'ces êtres supérieurs, les uniques détenteurs des connaissances et des mystères'(p. 181). Information is no longer given to educate and instruct: its role is to feed consumerism. Information has a commercial not moral value. Thus the generation gap is not entirely the fault of parents. It has been exacerbated by rapid social change, making parents feel frustrated and unsure of their role. As a parent herself the author is sympathetic to their plight, and she records her dislike for pejorative and cruel expressions like 'mon vieux' and 'ma vieille', which are used by some young people to refer to their mothers and fathers (p. 37). Even though teenagers know that their parents are not old in years, they represent 'un hier dont les jeunes n'ont rien à foutre'(p. 38).

One of the effects of the generation gap is that children see the past differently from their parents and grandparents.The Resistance movement of the last war is a case in point. Even though her own generation did not take part in it, they are able to identify with it. The grandparents of today's children actually lived through it. For her children's generation, however, the Resistance is part of History (with a capital H), like Joan of Arc and Napoleon. It does not impinge on their own experience. They are the children of the Algerian war. But nobody speaks of that war. They would have been aged between six and ten at the time. They may have older brothers or sisters who speak of it, but it does not have the same patriotic ring as the Resistance, evoking instead bitterness and national humiliation. Thus the young have a different perspective on modern French history.

The music of the young is a constant reminder that the generation gap exists. It is incomprehensible, according to Marie, because 'cette musique est la seule chose qui appartienne absolument à cette génération'(p. 34). Their music transports the young into a dream world of their own and, throughout the Western world, it has become a new lingua franca, displacing the written word. Teenagers in Europe or the United States are capable of exhibiting a near religious zeal for music. Marie concludes that if one cannot understand the music of the young one cannot communicate with them. She has had young people from all over the world in the flat and they all speak the same language of music—folk songs, Jimi Hendrix, etc. She recalls a camping holiday in Canada with her children. A group of motorbikers approached the camp. Marie thought there would be violence, but Charlotte's boyfriend, Alain, started to strum his guitar and Charlotte started to hum. The ice was broken and the motorbikers and campers became friends. 'C'était la musique qui avait ouvert les portes'(p. 41)

A critical appraisal of youth

i) The strength of youth

Marie is aware of young people's positive qualities, especially her own children's. Charlotte, we are told, likes poetry and has a vivid and playful imagination. She spends time in quiet meditation, although she is not secretive. The other daughter, Dorothée, is a natural *contestataire* , or rebel. She even rebels against the idea of rebellion, and her mother imagines her as a beautiful and intelligent technocrat. She also has an acute sense of justice. Marie describes her children as 'vivants', 'intelligents' and 'indépendants'(p. 15). The life of teenagers is described as 'confuse, multiple, simple, vraie, dure'(p. 16). Although Charlotte is a worry to her mother, she is capable of being calm, reasonable, thoughtful and behaving with maturity. She is on the pill, but decides not to sleep with her boyfriend because she does not consider herself old enough to enter into a sexual relationship. Marie remarks: 'Elle m'a dit cela si paisiblement, avec une telle sagesse que j'en ai été bouleversée'(p. 22). The capacity of the young to daydream is portrayed sympathetically as a natural part of adolescence. Above all else her children show her love, affection and trust and, although there are periods of conflict and non-communication, especially with Charlotte, she succeeds in bridging the generation gap by becoming both a mother and a friend to them. Young people can also show self-reliance and a sense of responsibility. In spite of having a difficult relationship with her parents, Sarah 'assume ses problèmes'(p. 87). She is a well-adjusted young woman who is always ready to help others. For example, she is a steadying influence on Charlotte and, being a year older, helps her with schoolwork. Young people can also show intellectual rigour. Thus Dorothée resists being sucked into the nihilism of the Americans who take over the flat, thanks to her training in modern mathematics which gives her a sense of proportion and reality. Young people can also show self-awareness and think for themselves: Marie's children and their friends see through the intellectual cant and moral emptiness of the young Americans. On a more general level, May '68 also represented a sudden outburst of protest by youth against the rigidities of French society, often referred to as 'la société bloquée'.

ii) The temptation of 'l'univers débile'

The words *débile* and *débilité* are recurrent terms used by a number of the young people who frequent the flat. It is significant that most of her children's friends and acquaintances are of middle-class origin. They have received the benefits of a *lycée* education, which has given them a veneer of intellectual sophistication. They often have time on their hands to think and daydream, but lack self-discipline because of their spoilt upbringing. The temptation is to withdraw into the world of *débilité* . It is difficult to pin down the exact meaning because it is a catch-all word that expresses both a critique of society and a personal philosophy of life. It has a negative sense when used of parents and of society in general, denoting stupidity and hollowness. By contrast, when it is used of themselves, it acquires, in a perverse way, a connotation of pseudo-romantic world weariness that allows them to pose as society's outcasts, rejoicing in the splendid isolation of their own egos. The term epitomises the desire to "opt out". However, Marie sees through the posturing and bravado and exposes the root causes of *débilité* : hypocrisy born of inverted bourgeois snobbery, moral weakness, a refusal to face reality, emotional insecurity, selfishness and self-destructiveness. Even a sensible young person like Charlotte is influenced by 'l'univers débile' through associating with the Clamart group. Marie decides to write down her thoughts in the first place as a way of releasing some of the anxiety and tension which Charlotte caused her.

Less attractive by far than Tom Wolfe's "Pump House Gang", the Clamart garage crowd are described as a handful of scum, 'contestant une société de laquelle ils ne savent pas se passer'(p. 17). They scrounge off their parents and, having abandoned their studies, do small odd jobs which their parents have got for them through contacts, and which should rightfully go to young workers who are on the dole. They drift in and out of jobs, all the while criticising the *débilité* of people they work with. Despite the pretence of equality between the sexes in the group, the girls remain sex objects for the boys in the same way that women are objects for their 'pères débiles'(p. 18). The girls may talk the language of feminism, but in practice accept a subservient role. When Françoise is made pregnant by one of the group, she has to turn to Marie for advice and help. The Clamarts are 'gosses de riches' who play at being workers and act as reactionaries (p. 18). The anarchism they espouse is pure dilettantism, and they remain fundamentally egotists. Their idea of community is one in which each one behaves as he likes. They are unable to agree on a code of behaviour and are devoid of political or social conscience. They are characterised instead by a 'vacuité vertigineuse', by indolence, and by indifference to everything outside themselves (p. 23).

The members of the Dalton gang are also devotees of the cult of *débilité* . In their private jargon, *débilité* has the aforementioned paradoxical meaning. Everything outside their world is *débile* and they, in their world, are equally *débile* . The more the member of the group is *débile* , the higher his standing. Marie tries to reason with them by arguing that man is a social being, and that if one opts out the initial euphoria of freedom will give way to despair. They refuse to take a political stand, saying that 'la révolution, c'est débile'(p. 70). One of the group, Jean-François, 'entretient la culture dialectique de la débilité'(p. 70). He has read and talked a lot with his mother, who is a cultured and intelligent woman. He argues that drugs are the only valid form of escape from society. Marie objects that suicide is a more courageous form of protest. She tells Jean-François that because he has a superficial view of society and cannot accept the notion of social order he is driven to nihilism. She writes of the Daltons: 'Ils piétinent dans le carcan des anciens systèmes usés jusqu'à la corde'(p. 73).

The most extreme form of *débilité* is provided by the group of young Americans. 'Tout se décomposait à leur contact. La crasse, la gentillesse et le néant régnaient'(p. 118). Marie comments that the despair of young Americans is greater than that of young Europeans. The former have grown up in the most consumer-oriented society in the world, and the disgust they feel for the system makes them either apathetic or dangerous. The apolitical majority of young Americans need to become politically aware. Their socialism is redolent of Christian charity and their communities are like churches. The young Americans who settle in the flat are neither Maoists, *gauchistes* , communists, Christians of any sort, hooligans nor thieves. They are simply unhappy adolescents, 'des paumés'(p. 131). Some beg in the streets, and Marie comments: 'Ils confondaient ouvriers et débiles'(p. 131). The Americans ape poverty and Marie brands their posturing a form of inverted snobbery. When she recalls that there are so many people in the world living in abject poverty through no fault of their own, she is filled with outrage at their behaviour. In their desire to rebel against their families they admire indiscriminately whatever runs counter to their upbringing.

An example of the hypocrisy of the young is provided by the incident of the stolen silverware. Her children and their friends protest that to call in the police would be like fraternising with the enemy. She objects that they do not mind her soiling her hands by earning her living from society so long as they are not tainted by contact with the guardians of social order. She says of their attitude: 'Je crois qu'ils ne sont que des bourgeois qui n'acceptent pas la forme bourgeoise. La forme seulement'(p. 158).

iii) The exploitation of youth

The author records that, when she was an adolescent, teenagers did not attract attention. Now they represent 'un fameux marché'(p. 107). They are an important market within consumer society, and the image of youth is systematically exploited by advertising companies to sell products. Catch phrases like 'la cigarette qui fait jeune' and 'la boisson des jeunes' are used to lure buyers (p. 144). "Youth" has become synonymous with "modern". The advertising industry has generated a consumer appetite in young people. From adolescence onwards they are aware of the economic and cultural forces which manipulate them, but they are not mature enough to resist.

Youth is also exploited politically. The events of May '68 worried the government, which set about defusing the students' potential for making revolution. Marie quotes the Prime Minister's 1969 declaration: 'Notre société aura le visage de la jeunesse'(p. 143). The problem is that young people no longer have faith in family, country, religion or school. They despise the society in which they live. They reject politics but lack the confidence in themselves to invent an alternative society. They are swept hither and thither. The condition of *anomie* seems to affect mainly middle-class children. Working-class adolescents also have difficulty in adjusting to society, but their malaise manifests itself differently. Either they rebel by becoming politically active or they conform. Some become agitators or hooligans. According to Marie, the authorities exploited the hooligan element to discredit the *gauchistes* in May '68. Fascist agitators would start a fight with hooligans and then make a quick escape by car. The hooligans would then side with the left-wing students against the fascistic organisation, Ordre Nouveau. This would be reported in the press as 'bagarres entre gauchistes et forces de l'ordre'(p. 153). Even though the authorities knew the real facts, the *gauchistes* became identified in the public mind with the hooligan element in society.

The most lethal form of exploitation is in the peddling of drugs to the young, a practice which Marie vilifies as 'un sordide marché aux esclaves, [...] la plus laide exploitation du consommateur'(p. 65). Marie examines the measures governments could adopt to stem the drug trade by buying up, for example, the poppy fields in Asia or by helping poor countries to make a livelihood from other cash crops. She suspects that governments do not care enough: 'Où sont les intérêts là-dedans ? Où sont les salauds ?'(p. 65). The problem is a very real one for Marie, who fears that Charlotte, under the influence of the Clamart group, may be tempted to experiment with drugs (p. 23). Many of the young people she befriends either know friends or acquaintances on drugs, or have themselves used drugs. One of the most tragic examples is Lakdar, who only finally came off heroine when he saw his girlfriend become a physical wreck before his very eyes because of her own heroine addiction.

Structure, style and characterisation

The story of *La Clé sur la porte* has three interlinking narrative threads. In the first we find descriptions of Marie's children and their friends, the Clamarts, the Daltons, the Bragnoli sisters, the Americans, Françoise, Sophia, Genéviève, Moussia and Lakdar. In the second there are a series of recollections of Marie's childhood in Algeria. The third thread consists of a series of sociological, political and ethical reflections on the problems facing contemporary youth. The story begins with an explanation of what motivates writers to write in the first place. Marie implies it provides a cathartic experience which enables the writer to sublimate the worries and tensions that arise in life. Thus *La Clé sur la porte* is inspired by her youngest daughter's flirtation with a group of dropouts who dabble in drugs, while the novel concludes with a prose poem written by Moussia as a way of exorcising through language the psychic pain she suffers from the knowledge that her mother had wanted to have her aborted. Moussia's poem is an extraordinarily mature piece of writing for an adolescent, combining as it does detachment and despair, tenderness and violence, refinement of expression and vulgarity. Indeed, the pretence that she is faithfully transcribing the words of someone else is hard to sustain. Written from the mother's point of view, the poem catalogues abortion-inducing techniques (the rough sport of moto-cross and the use of drugs like quinine) and uses violent images to describe the destruction of the foetus ('arrachement', 'coup de boutoir', etc.) The sense of revulsion provoked by the foetus ('ordure', 'montagne de rebuts') is counterpoised by terms of endearment for the unborn child ('ma mignonne', 'ma belle enfant', etc.) The effect is to underline the conflicting emotions and moral dilemmas generated by abortion.

The style of the novel is personal, passionate, rich in humour and emotion, providing a serious and colourful portrayal of contemporary youth. The story follows very closely the author's own life, and the reader may well ask whether he is reading fiction or autobiography. The work is clearly referred to as a *roman* by the publisher of the Livre de Poche edition, although Cardinal writes more ambiguously in *Autrement dit*: : 'J'ai besoin d'être la femme de chacun de mes livres.' [9] However, the story is not purely autobiographical. Her personal experiences as a mother have been distilled to capture the spirit of youth, so it is legitimate to retain the generic title of novel.

There is no coherent plot as such, rather a series of vignettes, pen portraits, snatches of dialogue and general reflexions. The structure follows very loosely the form of a diary. A whole kaleidoscope of characters as well as places is evoked, particularly those connected with her own childhood. There is a strong whiff of nostalgia, with the conjuring up of bitter-sweet memories. The claustrophobic atmosphere of the overcrowded flat is punctuated by recollections of her Algerian childhood and holidays spent in North America. Thus the story unfolds against the background of three continents. Most of the characters only occur once in the story. Apart from her children, Lakdar is the one notable exception . The author is more concerned with giving a collective portrait of youth than with offering an individual, in-depth character study.

Because of the use of the first person singular, the author has an immediate and personal impact on the reader. It is the language of a confidante, friend, but especially that of a mother. Cardinal is very good at expressing intimacy and emotion: for example, the scene in which she cradles her daughter who has awoken from a nightmare and whom she calls 'ma petite caille', 'ma merveille', 'ma chatonne'(p. 9). Of her son, she writes with simple directness: 'Il aime être en famille. Il m'aime'(p. 13). She deploys stylistic devices in an effective and economical way to obtain different effects. Thus the 1950s (p. 35) and the postwar era (p. 80) are conjured up by a collage of names, events and places, and reminiscences of a trip to metropolitan Paris and its monuments are punctuated by the names of fashion houses and expensive delicatessens also visited (pp. 162-4). To convey the stereotyped character of her husband's friends in Montreal, she notes their age and personal appearance with the curt formulae of a police description (p. 96). By cleverly juxtaposing the sacred liturgy of the Tridentine Mass and her own daydreams, the author underlines graphically the tension between her conventional religious upbringing and her unconventional and carefree spirit (pp. 104-105).

Apart from occasional literary flourishes like Moussia's poem and the description of her visit with her mother to the cemetery, the style reflects spoken French. The shortened form *ça* is invariably used instead of *cela* , and is also found, as in spoken language, in place of proper nouns: for example, 'ça ne court pas les rues', meaning in this context, 'you don't see many good-looking young men about'(p. 17). Among examples of slang words and expressions are the following: *pognon* and *fric* (dough), *dingueries* (tomfoolery), *n'avoir rien à foutre de* (not to give a damn about), *boulots merdiques* (dirty jobs), *connerie* (boloney), *Amerloques* (Yanks), *raconter des salades* (to talk poppycock), *vachement* (bloody), *flic* (cop), *dégueulasse* (disgusting), *se pointer* (to pop up), *se coller les jetons* (to get the jitters), *tambouille* (nosh), *faire chier quelqu'un* (to give someone the pip), *ras le bol* (to have had it up to here) and *mec* (bloke).

Examples of political slang reflect the impact of May '68 at the time of writing the novel. Thus we find communists, reactionaries and fascists described respectively as *cocos* , *réacs* and *fafs* . Of particular interest is Cardinal's grasp of the nuances of slang words in fashion among the young: already mentioned have been *ma vieille* and *mon vieux* for parents, and words like *débile* and *débilité* . By her efforts to convey the language and speech patterns of adolescents, she avoids being falsely literary. The colloquial style that results is more appropriate to the subject matter in hand, capturing as it does the nonconformist spirit of youth.

NOTES

(1)   *Autrement dit*   (Paris, 1977), p. 162.

(2)   Ibid. p. 202

(3)   Ibid. p. 62

(4)   B. Vercier, J. Lecarme, *La littérature en France depuis 1968* (Paris, 1982), p. 235.

(5)   John Ardagh, *The New France. A Society in Transition 1945-1973*   (Harmondsworth, 1973), p. 438.

(6)   Philippe Lasselain, 'La maturité politique de l'étudiant', in M. Beaujour, J. Ehrmann, *La France contemporaine* (Paris, 1966), p. 62.

(7)   Bernard E.Brown, *Protest in Paris: Anatomy of a Revolt* (New Jersey, 1974), p. 44.

(8)   P. Apel-Muller, M.Jauffret, *Les Enfants du Siècle* (Paris, 1986), p. 20.

(9)   *Autrement dit* , p. 86.

CONCLUSION

The novels raise a number of important issues: child deprivation and delinquency, the responsibility of adults towards children, the generation gap and the nature of modern youth culture. In the end the reader is left with three main questions: "What characterises the style of these two novels ?"; "What picture do they give of post-war French society ?"; "How convincingly do they portray the psychological and moral development of children and adolescents ?"

Chiens perdus sans collier is full of dramatic incident, changes of location, many characters the reader is able to identify with and even admire, a fast-moving plot and a happy ending. If it is strong on pathos it is also somewhat lacking in humour. It is a novel about children not for children and addresses the reader's social conscience, drawing him into a world with which he is probably quite unfamiliar. No matter how sensitively Cesbron draws his child characters, he cannot know them as intimately as Cardinal knows her adolescent subjects. Cesbron was born into a different social milieu from that of the children he portrays, whereas Cardinal is writing about her own children. Because she knows her subjects so intimately she is able to capture their foibles and little hypocrisies. This helps to account for her greater use of irony than Cesbron. Nevertheless, like Cesbron's novel, *La Clé sur la porte* is lacking in humour, perhaps because it reflects the concern and anxiety felt by the author for her children's welfare at a vulnerable stage in their lives.

French society forms an important backcloth to both novels. *Chiens perdus sans collier* depicts some of the weakest and least articulate members of society: deprived working-class children who are the victims of adult neglect and abuse and the passive recipients of society's welfare and charity. The adult characters supply the political and social sub-text: the strengths and weaknesses of *l'Etat-providence* , the Welfare State; the social inequalities that arise from disparities of wealth and power; and the social ostracism of marginal groups and slum communities. In the two decades or so between the publication of Cesbron's novel and of *La Clé sur la porte* , France underwent significant political and social change: there was an economic and population boom which allowed for the expansion of the educational system, the growth of an increasingly affluent and media-saturated society, the rise of a youth or teenage culture and the erosion of traditional family life and of parental authority. The postwar complacency of the bourgeoisie was severely shaken by the events of May. The subjects of Cardinal's novel are middle-class adolescents, the future bearers and perhaps even moulders of their culture. They have internalised many of the social and political conflicts of French and Western society and are therefore more accurate barometers of social change than Cesbron's characters. It is interesting to note also that both Cesbron and Cardinal come from roughly the same middle-class stratum of society, and both had a Catholic upbringing. Cesbron remained a Catholic, while Cardinal has rejected the religion of her youth and has even become anticlerical. In this they illustrate the long history of division in France between Catholics and lay anticlericals. What is particularly significant, however, is the way both writers expose the selfishness and hypocrisy of their own class. Cesbron attacks the values of the bourgeoisie in the name of the Gospel; Cardinal does the same from a secular humanist standpoint.

*****

Cesbron brings into focus the two primary influences affecting the moral and psychological development of the child: parents and peer group. The children in *Chiens perdus sans collier* suffer from a double handicap; they are either orphans or have inadequate parents, and their peer group fosters delinquency. The novel explores the different forms of maltreatment children suffer at the hands of adults: emotional (the Deroux couple's treatment of Alain), social (Doublet's disdain for deprived children) and moral (the attempted sexual abuse of Alain in a Paris park). The tension between children and step-parents is also highlighted (Colombo, for example, whose stepfather regularly beats up his mother). Adult characters like Lamy try to supply the care and moral guidance the children's own parents have failed to provide—hence the symbolism of the dog collar in the title. The peer group remains an important factor in fostering the moral development of the child because the experience of role-taking within the group transforms the perceptions of rules from external authoritarian commands to internal principles. Thus Marc's sense of loyalty to his gang leader, although misplaced, represents an important stage in the development of his moral consciousness. The children display different degrees of moral awareness. For Merlerin, being good is a ploy to obtain rewards, although he is capable of altruism, as manifested in his protectiveness towards Mammy's son. Marc and Alain show a more acute moral sense than Merlerin because they behave in order to obtain the approval of a person whom they respect (Lamy). Paradoxically it is Paulo, the most delinquent of all the boys, who displays the highest form of moral awareness when he finally confesses to the theft of the car and the assault on Robert. He does so in order not to lose his self-respect. Doublet refuses to recognise that deprived and delinquent youngsters can show a high degree of moral discretion and regards them as motivated to conform simply out of fear of punishment. In his eyes they can never develop beyond a primitive stage of moral awareness, and are condemned to remain permanently immature. He represents the blindness of the worldly, but his cynicism is confounded by the trust Lamy shows towards children in care. Of course the children at Terneray are not little angels—witness how those who have parents taunt the orphans. Yet there is nothing abnormal in such behaviour; most children are capable of showing cruelty. Indeed, despite their obvious social handicaps, Alain, Marc and the other boys are children who have the potential to grow up into well-adjusted adults. Cesbron's approach is not merely compassionate but also optimistic. He rejects the notion that delinquency leads inevitably to criminality, and it is therefore all the sadder when a youth like Paulo, who is capable of showing moral maturity, seems firmly embedded in patterns of petty crime.

*****

The major characteristics of adolescence are portrayed in *La Clé sur la porte* . It is set at the crucial time when, while still needing their parents, the young strive to become emotionally independent of them. Marie has to walk a tightrope between being a mother and therefore a figure of authority on the one hand, and a friend and confidante on the other. She understands the trauma involved in breaking free of one's parents because her own struggle for independence was slow, painful and only complete with her mother's death. Adolescence is also a time of emotional upheaval and behavioural contradictions. In particular, it is a time of sexual awakening. The danger of an unwanted pregnancy, like Françoise's, is a cause of parental anxiety, and Marie is concerned about Charlotte. Outside the home the major influences on the adolescent are school, the contemporary youth culture and especially peer groups. Adolescence is also a period of growth in maturity and sense of personal responsibility, as seen in Sarah's concern for Charlotte. It is a time when the young begin to evaluate themselves: Charlotte decides that she is not ready for a sexual relationship with her boyfriend. The adolescent has to grapple with his or her own identity and acquire an adult status in society, which is conferred by a vocation or job: Marie's eldest son, who is struggling to make a career in the film industry, experiences frustration and loneliness born of insecurity. Idealism, which is another characteristic of youth, often leads to a (superficial) rejection of society. The idealism of Marie's children and their friends is directed at global issues—racialism, famine, the abuse of human rights, etc. They find it difficult to channel their ideals into traditional organisations like political parties. This is partly due to inexperience, but there are specific cultural factors operating in the case of French children. The ethos of the French school is too bound up with passing exams and not enough with the moral and social education of the young person. This is seen as almost the sole responsibility of parents. Adolescents and young adults in France also tend to be more emotionally and materially dependent on their parents than their counterparts in Britain; the French family is more close-knit and young people often live at home until marriage, even if they are full-time students or in work.

The reader is left with the impression that traditional family life in France is in crisis, but he may equally ask how typical are the families portrayed. Marie's own family is unlike the average two-parent household (although the number of single-parent families in France is growing). Her flat is a magnet for emotionally deprived middle-class adolescents who are the victims of selfish parents and of what is called the permissive society. Marie Cardinal's catalogue of drug addiction, abortion and family conflict errs on the side of pessimism. She wants to be a modern and enlightened mother and shows a courageous willingness to let her children discover for themselves what is right for them, as long as it is done under her own supervision. Has her decision to keep "the key in the door" helped them to achieve independence more effectively than a more insular family would have, or has it made adolescence a more testing time than it might otherwise have been ? This is the question Marie leaves the reader to ponder.

GLOSSARY OF TERMS

The aim of this series is to provide "Europ-Assistance", extending to North Africa, in all areas of difficulty. Hence the following English equivalents or explanations are offered for cases where a modern history book, a slang dictionary or the new *Collins Robert French Dictionary* are unavailable or unhelpful. Popular language is notoriously difficult to translate in a way satisfactory to all, and our approach has been to avoid the archaic and the overly vulgar. No doubt some terms that are asterisked appear a little euphemistic, and others are undeniably dated. May we rely on the reader's no doubt extensive vocabulary to supply any deficiencies ?

*****

AB2 — a *baccalauréat* combination of French, modern languages and economics.

Bagnole (CE34, CA125, etc.) — Banger, motor

baiser (CA53) — bonk, screw*.

balles (CE96) — francs.

baquet à l'oreillard (CA14) — baccalauréat (misheard!).

baratin (CA146) — Chat, line, patter.

barbe, la (CE117, etc.) — boring, boring; or: "not likely".

barrer, se (CA32, CE61, etc.) — blow, split, etc. Imperative: "on your bike", "get lost".

berzingue, à tout (CA79) — at full belt, blast.

besef (CA174) — very (transcription of Arabic).

bicot (CE64) — wog, darkie (in context, N. African Arab).

bidule (CE95) — thingy.

blairer (CA185) — in the negative, stand, abide.

blagues, sans (CE123) — expression of incredulity akin to a certain tennis player's 'You *cannot* be serious'.

bol, en avoir ras le (CA121) — to be browned* off with.

bordel (CE203) — in context, "crummy show".

boulot (CA49) — job.

bourlinguer (CA93) — to knock about.

Bread and Pupett [*sic*] (CA93) — late sixties theatre group.

buffet (CE157) — stomach, below the belt.

Cafard (CA51) — blues, being "down".

caïd — chief.

60

camé (CA50)	dopehead.
canasson (CA183)	horse, nag.
char, arrêter ton (CA147)	belt up.
charger (CE63)	overplay, go over the top.
chat! (CE124)	Tick, you're on, etc.
chialer (CE211)	bawl, howl, "greet".
chibania (CA174)	old (Arabic).
chiche que (CE64)	bet you won't, dare you to.
chier, faire (CA142)	to brown* off. Very strong here, often meaning merely "to exaggerate". 'Fais pas chier, papa ! ' does not normally lead to loss of privileges
chiottes (CA57)	bog, loo, john.
clebs (CE210)	dog.
Clemenceau (CE99)	a reference to the politician (1841-1929).
cloque (CA31)	pudding club, up the stick.
colle (CA47)	detention.
con (CE16)	pillock (as adj., idiotic, daft); 'à la con' (CE187) = stupid wee ...
couillon (CE159)	asshole.
crins, à tous (CA114)	mad keen, fanatical.
croquignolet (CA99)	cute.
crotte de nez (CE118)	snotter.
cuistot (CE100)	chef.
culs-terreux (CE123)	peasants.
curetons (CE118)	Holy Willies, "Jesus-creepers".
Dalton, les (CA73)	A reference to the four convict brothers, all looking the same but of different heights, who are the traditional enemies of the cartoon hero Lucky Luke.
défoncer, se (CA51)	trip.
dégueulasse (CA55)	crappy*, disgusting.
dégueuler (CA127)	puke.
démerder, se (CE105)	sort, work out, arrange.
dent, avoir la (CA126)	be hungry.
Emmerder (tr.) (CE15)	to despise*.
(refl.) (CE146)	to be bored stiff or, negated, to be having a great time, often with sexual connotations (CA174).
emmerdeurs (CE258)	stirrers.
engueulade (CE146)	bollocking.
Feignant (CE123)	idler, lazybones.
fin du fin, *le* (CA69)	really ace.
flinguer, se (CA77)	do o.s. in.
flipper comme un dingue (CA69)	get incredibly depressed.
foirer (CA80)	screw* up.

foutaises (CA102)	crap.
frangin(e) (CE50, 58, etc.)	bruv, bro. / sis
fricky (CA73 *et passim*)	in-crowd *argot* that takes on almost any nuance of fashion or "coolness". Or can mean (CA155) kitsch, tacky. Has not survived outside this social circle.
fringues (CA73)	clothes, gear.
Garçon de lait (CA123)	grisly pun based on the fact that a *cochon de lait* is a sucking pig.
godillots (CA123)	big boots, "Docs"
gueule, se fendre la (CE150)	to wet* o.s. laughing
gueule, se foutre de la (CA156)	thumb one's nose at, take the Michael*.
Inch Allah (CA172)	May God's will be done.
J.E.C. (CA110)	Jeunesse étudiante chrétienne
Jésus-flexions (CE123)	v. forced pun on *génuflexions* —something like "Jeez-bends".
Machin (CE74, CA163)	`Thingmy.
Maman Papier (CE13)	pun based on "maman, papa".
mariejeanne (CA97)	obviously, marijuana.
marrant (CE211)	a howl, kill.
merdique (CA49)	crappy*.
Mickey (CA104, CE86)	Mickey Mouse.
minette (CA84)	dolly.
Nana (CA109)	ditto.
nichons (CA35)	boobs, tits.
nippes (CA73)	clothes.
nounou (CE150)	nursey.
Overney, "Pierrot" (CA155)	Maoist militant killed outside a Paris Renault factory in February 1972. A ferocious cartoon in *Charlie Hebdo* showed his funeral procession headed by their brand new car mouthing the publicity slogan: 'Bonjour ! Je suis la Renault 5.'
Pagaille (CA47)	anarchy, madhouse.
papelards (CE13)	papers.
papier cul (CA95)	bog roll.
parles, tu (CE67, etc.)	expression of doubt, e.g. "no chance", "no way".
patelin (CA157)	village.
paumé (CA131)	loser.

P.C.V. (CA119)	reversed charges (*à percevoir*).
pénard (CE279)	relaxed, laid back.
piaule (CA83)	room, "pad".
pieds, casser les (CA187)	brass* off, get on s.o.'s wick*.
pince (CA147)	mitt.
piquer (CE42)	half-inch, nick.
pipelette (CA82)	concierge.
plafonner (CE229)	mark time.
planer (CA54)	trip.
planquer (CE275)	hide, stash, "plank".
pognon + fou (CA186)	(cost) the earth, a bomb.
poilant (CE211)	funny.
pointer, se (CA59)	to show up.
pompes (CA77)	shoes.
pompiers, faire des (CA120)	fellate*.
poux, plein de (CE156)	fleabag.
Râler (CE80)	grumble, complain.
ralouf (CA174)	pig, dirty beast (Arabic).
raton (CE87)	*can* mean "wog" or "coon", but in context probably "*ra* coon", the *raton laveur* .
rombier (CE108)	old-fashioned, starchy, boring
roses, pot aux (CA120)	guilty secret
rustines (CE9)	inner tube patches (typical contents of a boy's pocket!)
Salades (CA27, 62)	a line (that one shoots s.o.), load of old cobblers, mess.
salope (CE144)	bitch.
saloperie (CE216)	filth.
sapes (CA75)	clothes.
sapeur Camember (CA165)	dumb soldier (a very early cartoon character).
Tabac, passage à (CA152)	thumping, bashing.
tabla (CA13)	xylophone.
tacot (CA125)	banger.
Tot<u>o-la-f</u> iente (CE106)	Mucky Pup (the letters "Olaf" are in the middle)
trouille bleue, avoir une (CA169)	to be dead* scared, petrified
tuile (CA182)	piece of bad news, sickener.
UDR, municipalité (CA110)	with a right-wing council.
Verni (CE267)	lucky, in clover.
vue, en mettre plein la (CA71)	to con.
Zazou (CA82)	cool, *branché* individual.
zéro, on les avait à (CA125)	we were sweating cobs, scared wit*less.

SELECT BIBLIOGRAPHY

For background reading and reference, the following are useful:—

Ardagh, J.

The New France. A Society in Transition 1945-1977, (Harmondsworth, Penguin, 1981), pp. 465-521. [Examines the family, school and youth culture in France].

La Documentation
Française

Les Institutions sociales en France (La Documentation Française, 1980), pp. 611-643. [Discusses the Child Welfare Services, juvenile delinquency and the law].

Reynaud, Jean-Daniel,
Grafmeyer, Yves

Français, qui êtes-vous? Des essais et des chiffres (La Documentation Française, 1981), pp. 285-339. [Useful insights into the French view of authority, the generation gap, the evolution of the family, the role of women and the contemporary youth culture].

For further reading on Cesbron and Cardinal, recommended are:—

Barlow, M.

Gilbert Cesbron, témoin de la tendresse de Dieu . Paris, Laffont, 1965.

Cardinal, M.

Les Mots pour le dire . Paris, Grasset et Fasquelle, 1983.

Lavigne, C.

"Cardinal, Marie" in *Dictionnaire des littératures de la langue française* , edited by J.-P. de Beaumarchais, Daniel Coty and Alain Rey (Paris: Bordas, 1984), pp. 369-370.

O'Flaherty, K.

The Novel in France 1945-1965 : A general survey, (Cork: University of Cork Press, 1973), pp.28-33 [on Cesbron].